Honoring the Light of the Child

Activities to Nurture Peaceful Living Skills in Young Children

SONNIE MCFARLAND

Peace Music for children—now available online! (See page 119)

SHINING MOUNTAINS PRESS

BUENA VISTA, COLORADO

Although the author and publisher have made every effort to ensure the
accuracy and completeness of information contained in this book, we assume
no responsibility for errors, inaccuracies, omissions, or any inconsistency herein.
Any slights of people, places, or organizations are unintentional.

LCCN: 2008904884
ISBN: 978-0-9754887-2-0 [0-9754887-2-4]
1st printing 2004 • 2nd printing 2005 • Updated 3rd printing 2020

Printed and bound in the United States of America.

Previously printed and sold with music CD: 2008 • 2010 • 2012 • 2014 • 2015 • 2017 (ISBN: 978-0-9754887-3-7)

**ATTENTION CORPORATIONS, UNIVERSITIES, COLLEGES, AND PROFES-
SIONAL ORGANIZATIONS:** Quantity discounts are available on bulk purchases of
this book for educational, gift purposes, or as premiums for increasing magazine sub-
scriptions or renewals. Special books or book excerpts can also be created to fit specific
needs. For information, please contact Shining Mountains Press, P.O. Box 4155, Buena
Vista, CO 81211; (719) 207-2227. www.ShiningMountainsPress.com

Dedication

I dedicate this book to the inner light of love in children everywhere. I offer this book as a gift to the children and sincerely pray that it will inspire and assist educators in their important work of encouraging children to fulfill their greatest potential.

All people, especially children, when manifesting the greater Self within, are shining mountains glowing with eternal promise.

—DR. JIM MCFARLAND

About the Cover

There is a special story to tell about the beautiful child who appears on the cover of this book. As you will note, she is wearing a small yellow felt circle on her chest which represents her love light. The concept of the love light had been introduced to her in class and she was encouraged to wear a Love Light Pin whenever she felt love in her heart.

On this particular occasion she had taken the Love Light Pin home over the weekend and was joyfully wearing it outside when her mother released a butterfly that spontaneously landed on the child's hand as you see it.

Look closely and you can literally see her love light shining through her eyes. A picture is worth a thousand words!

About the Music

In this edition of *Honoring the Light of the Child*, I am happy to collaborate with my dear friend and talented musician, Pat Yonka, to provide online MP3s of the peace songs suggested in this book, as well as additional songs related to peace activities. The song lyrics can be found starting on page 119. A link to the MP3 files can be found at **https://bit.ly/36Ylh5sMusicPeace.**

Pat is not only a talented musician, but also a compassionate peacemaker. She beautifully combines these talents and inspires peace through her music, which she sees as a universal language. The melody and the manner in which the song is sung speak to people of all languages. Music connects us through the beat as we are connected by the beat of our hearts. The heartbeat within each of us is the same, regardless of our nationality.

Let Us All Sing!

Table of Contents

Foreword

S ONNIE MCFARLAND is a pioneer in the teaching of peace to young children. Her work was an inspiration to me during the years I was preparing my book, *Nurturing the Spirit in Non-Sectarian Classrooms.* Since that publication in 1996, Sonnie has expanded and refined the details of her series of activities, so that with this book, they can be easily used by other teachers. And they should be. As I am writing this, amid the world turmoil of 2003, it seems that practicing peace is the most important experience we can give to our children.

Some readers may wonder why it is necessary to design specific lessons on love, kindness, compassion and tolerance. They may feel that preparing a peaceful environment and modeling peaceful behavior is sufficient for guiding three through six year-old children. From my own experience as a child in school, I know that virtues such as these must be explicitly taught. With shame I recall that neither I, nor any of my other schoolmates, ever reached out to one particular girl in our class. She was a midget. We never invited her to play with us; we simply ignored her. Although we were taught in peaceful environments by women who valued peace, not one of them ever gave us a lesson on being sensitive to the feelings of others or including all our classmates in our activities.

Maria Montessori, in whose path Sonnie McFarland now walks, recognized a century ago the joy of repetition that children exhibit in the classroom. Montessori's materials invite young students to repeat and repeat each activity. The children delight in gradually mastering basic skills by returning to the same pieces of equipment or parallel lessons day after day. The very creative peace activities in this book offer children the same kind of comfortable repetition with frequent use of silence, songs, symbols and unique materials that embody peaceful thoughts and actions. There is no doubt in my mind that the repetition in these powerful lessons can make a significant difference in children's behavior.

Basic to the whole effort, however, is the nature of the teachers who use this program. In order to convey convincingly to their students the life changing meaning of these beautiful activities, teachers must do more than follow the procedures outlined in this book. They must be peaceful people themselves, whose commitment to peace proceeds from their own inner essence. This means that they take time in their busy schedules to nourish themselves spiritually, to reflect on their own strengths and weaknesses, to grow in patience and love, and as Montessori insisted, "to purify their hearts and render them burning with charity towards the child."

Ron Miller, whose well-known commitment to holistic education reflects his Montessori training, wrote recently, "If we are to teach peace, we need to learn to practice love, not only within intimate circles of families and friends, but in schools and in society and in the world at large. We need to transform society, reorganize our institutions, and expand our values, so that our culture favors caring, compassion, justice and love. No doubt it is a huge task. But it is our truest calling as human beings."

—ALINE D. WOLF

Preface

OVER THIRTY-FIVE YEARS ago, I read a book that changed the course of my life by igniting a flame in my heart that burns brightly to this day. This passion made parenting and teaching a pure joy and can be summed up in six simple words: "Honor the Light of the Child!"

In my experience the more I honor the light of love within children and reflect it back to them, the more they express love in cooperative and peaceful ways. Children come to the Earth as innocent spiritual beings bearing unique gifts to share with humanity. The ability of children to manifest these gifts to the fullest is greatly dependent on the significant adults in their lives.

The seeds of potential within children are similar to the seeds of potential within flowers. Just as a seed comes into the world with all it needs to grow and fulfill its destiny of becoming a certain type of flower, so children enter the world prepared to bloom into their own unique potential. However, both seeds and children must have certain conditions present if they are to bloom. Just as the gardener is responsible for providing the proper conditions for seeds to flourish, child educators, including parents, teachers, child counselors and anyone who works with and cares for young children, are responsible for providing nurturing environments for children to flourish.

The gardener must provide soil for the seeds to keep them warm, safe and secure. Similarly, child educators must provide physical safety to keep children warm, safe and secure.

The gardener must provide nutrients for the seeds to flourish and grow. Similarly, child educators must provide intellectual stimulation and encourage children to explore and create on an intellectual level.

The gardener must provide water so the seeds will soften, sprout and grow. Similarly, child educators must provide emotional environments for children that are safe enough for children to comfortably express themselves.

The gardener must place the seeds in a place where they get enough light to fill the plant with energy. Similarly, child educators must place children in the light. This is done by seeing and recognizing the light and potential within each child. When children experience their light reflected back to them, they flower. Just as the gardener plants a seed with a vision of the flower in mind, a child educator must continually honor the light or seed potential in each child.

The activities in this book provide a variety of opportunities for child educators to reflect love to the children, help them make conscious choices based on this and encourage them to live and work in a peaceful manner with others.

Acknowledgments

T HE FIRST PERSON I wish to acknowledge is my husband, Jim McFarland, who saw and shared the vision of possibility that lies deep within each child. In partnership we nurtured and enjoyed watching our two children, Christian and Jeannie, flower into peaceful, caring adults. I honor the light within them and thank them for showing me the joy of being a parent and teacher.

Special thanks go to the many children who have been in my classes for the past 35 years. Each has been my teacher, given me insight into the true nature and beauty of childhood, and sustained my hope for a more peaceful future.

I would like to acknowledge the faculty, staff and parents of the Montessori School of Denver who, for 23 years, worked with me to bring the best educational practices to the children. I would like to thank the 2001–2002 Primary teachers who opened their classrooms so I could bring the peace activities of this book to their students. I also acknowledge the parents of those students who enthusiastically supported this effort, graciously contributed comments and allowed me to publish their children's pictures.

I appreciate my colleagues throughout the educational community who support, encourage and participate in the important work of educating for peace. Dr. Betsy Coe, Pat Yonka stand out as two people who continually inspire and support me as we work together to define peace education and encourage educators to include it at all levels of education.

When I began this book, two special women stood at my side and made it possible for it to become a reality. From the beginning of this project Anita Albers and Kea Bardeen saw the value in this book and supported me throughout the process. Their generosity means so much!

As the book progressed, I couldn't have done it without the help of Judi Bauerlein, Janet Engel and Kelley Rand who reviewed and edited the manuscript. Abra Houston, Dave and Nancy Edwards contributed their artistic and technological skills to the project and served as cheerleaders throughout the writing of this book.

If there is one person who set the stage and tilled the soil to prepare the way for this book, it is Aline D. Wolf who so graciously wrote the Foreword. Her groundbreaking book *Nurturing the Spirit in Non-Sectarian Classrooms* clearly describes the importance of nurturing the spirit in children. I appreciate Aline for her vision, courage and clarity of thought.

Introduction

The Need to Educate
for a Culture of Peace

In every corner of the globe the anguished cries for peace can be heard. Millions of people cry in silence, carrying on their shoulders the burden of our tragic, never-ending drive toward confrontation, conflict and war. These same millions are also bearers of hope, of the unfulfilled quest for peace—a peace that will benefit us all according dignity to all human beings.[1]

THESE COMPELLING WORDS of Rigoberta Menchu Tum, the 1992 recipient of the Nobel Peace Prize, speak to the unquestionable need to transform our current global culture of violence to a global culture of peace.

All around we see suffering because so many people only know how to act from a paradigm of confrontation, conflict and war. They are unaware of alternative ways to respond to life. To transform our current culture of violence into a culture of peace, we must implement systematic and global education for peace. We must provide all children with the tools to interact from a position of respect, understanding and cooperation in order for a culture of peace to emerge. The activities in this book directly speak to these principles as they relate to young children.

The phrase "culture of peace" describes a society based on respect for peace at all levels, human rights and democratic principles. Federico Mayor, former Director General of the United Nations Educational, Scientific and Cultural Organization (UNESCO) and President of the Culture of Peace Foundation, used the culture of peace concept to organize and bring together peace efforts around the world. His vision and work ultimately influenced the United Nations to declare the years 2001–2011 as the *Decade for a Culture of Peace and Nonviolence for the Children of the World.*

According to UNESCO's description of its Culture of Peace Programme, the movement *"will take on a life of its own and become a self-sustaining irreversible transformation process from a culture of war to a culture of peace."*[2]

A primary component of this movement is to create systematic and global education for peace because teachers are the ones most directly involved in educating the children of the next generation. According to Janusz Symonides and Kishore Singh:

> *Education is at the heart of any strategy for the construction of a culture of peace. It is through education that the broadest possible introduction can be provided to the values, skills and knowledge which form the basis of respect for peace, human rights and democratic principles. It is an important means to eliminate suspicion, stereotypes and*

enemy images, and, at the same time, to promote the ideals of peace, tolerance and non-violence, and mutual appreciation among individuals, groups and nations. Education should not only strengthen the belief that peace is a fundamental value of humankind and create a non-violent mentality, but also mold an attitude of involvement and responsibility for matters relating to peace at local, national, regional and global levels.[3]

Indeed, teachers and parents play an important role in this process of transforming our culture of violence to a culture of peace. Through thoughtful guidance, teachers and parents are in a position to offer our children alternative ways of thinking, acting and being which is vital for this transformation to take place. Momentum is growing on a global level to create a global culture of peace.

In May of 1999, over 10,000 people, representing hundreds of organizations from around the world, came together in an historic gathering. This was held at The Hague in the Netherlands for the purpose of organizing a collaborative and cooperative effort to bring a culture of peace into reality. The agenda items resulting from The Hague Appeal for Peace Conference are documented in a pamphlet called *The Hague Agenda for Peace and Justice for the 21st Century.* The document includes 50 specific agenda items organized into four major strands:

1. Root Causes of War/Culture of Peace
2. International Humanitarian and Human Rights Law and Institutions
3. Prevention, Resolution and Transformation of Violent Conflict
4. Disarmament and Human Security

Of the 50 agenda items, I was happy to see that the first agenda item of the entire document is: *Educate for Peace, Human Rights and Democracy.* It states:

> In order to combat the culture of violence that pervades our society the coming generation deserves a radically different education—one that does not glorify war but educates for peace, nonviolence and international cooperation. The Hague Appeal for Peace has launched a world- wide campaign to empower people at all levels with the peacemaking skills of mediation, conflict transformation, consensus-building and non-violent social change. This campaign:
>
> • Insists that peace education be made compulsory at all levels of the education system.
>
> • Demands that education ministries (departments) systematically implement peace education initiatives at a local and national level.
>
> • Calls on development assistance agencies to promote peace education as a component of their teacher training and materials production.[4]

When I tell people that I educate for peace, they often give me a puzzled look and say, "What do you mean by peace?" Describing peace can be difficult. I was pleased when I came across Linda Groff and Paul Smoker's research in which they define peace at six different levels. I was most excited to discover that the work I do falls into the sixth or most basic level of peace: Holistic Inner and Outer Peace.[5]

1. Peace as Absence of War—Peace is defined as the time when there is no war. This model refers to either a national or an international level of peace. In our schools, we address this in our study of history and describe periods when there is no war as being times of peace.

2. Peace as the Balance of Forces in the International System—In this model, peace is seen as the balance of power needed to prevent war. The Cold War is an example of this level of peace. Again, in our study of history, credit for peace (no war) is given to the balance of international forces.

3. Peace as Negative Peace (No War) and Positive Peace (No Structural Violence)—This model includes the first level and goes further to define itself by the number of deaths avoided through the organization of various local, national and international structures. Structural violence is harm to the people, which is caused by certain policies of governments, institutions, businesses, etc. This level of peace is addressed through education when we teach professional ethics classes.

4. Feminist (Interpersonal) Peace: Macro and Micro Levels of Peace—This model moves to the interpersonal level and defines peace as treating all people with equality, from the individual to the global level. Beginning in the 1960's, education embraced minority studies such as women studies and black studies as a way to increase awareness and ensure equality among people.

5. Holistic Gaia-Peace: Peace with the Environment—This model includes the interpersonal aspects of the feminist model and additionally places a high value on the relationship of humans to bio-environmental systems. Peace with the environment is central to this model. Again, in the 1960's, education added environmental/ecological studies to the curriculum for the purpose of raising consciousness of the fragile balance between nature and humanity.

6. Holistic Inner and Outer Peace—This model stresses the centrality of inner peace, believing that all aspects of outer peace, from the individual to the environmental levels, must be based on inner peace. This level is only beginning to find its way into the educational system. It is the most comprehensive level and the one most likely to sustain a lasting peace at all levels.

As you will note in the next section of this Introduction, I based the activities in this book on a holistic model of peace called *The Flower of Peace Model.* The activities are designed to help children recognize their essential nature as love, maintain contact with this love, and consciously use it to make responsible choices in their interactions with other people and the environment. In my opinion, the more we recognize our inner nature as love and consciously center in this reality, the more inner peace we will experience because our outward actions reflect our internal reality. The more inner peace we have, the more harmony we will manifest in our relationships with other people and the environment.

Dr. Maria Montessori was one of the first educators to recognize the connection between seeing and responding to the intrinsic beauty and love within children and their ability to manifest their greatest potential and talents. She created an education model based on this realization:

> *. . . when the intrinsic value of the child's personality has been recognized and he has been given room to expand, as in the case of our school (when the child creates for himself an environment suited to his spiritual growth), we have had the revelation of an entirely new*

child whose astonishing characteristics are the opposite of those that had hitherto been observed. We may, therefore, assert that it would be possible, by the renewing of education, to produce a better type of man, a man endowed with superior characteristics as if belonging to a new race . . . Herein lies the part that education has to play in the struggle between war and peace, and not in its cultural content . . . [6]

Montessori went on to say that:

War would not be a problem at all for the soul of the new man: he would see it simply as a barbarous state, contrasting with civilization, an absurd and incomprehensible phenomenon. [7]

Educating for peace requires that we look to the root causes of war or violence as shown in the first agenda item coming out of The Hague Appeal for Peace. Dr. Montessori identified the root cause of war and violence as stemming from children's frustration and inability to know, love, express and fulfill themselves. She says that the first seeds of war are sown during the early childhood years if the adults do not recognize the intrinsic nature of the child.

When the independent life of the child is not recognized with its own characteristics and ends, when the adult man interprets these characteristics and ends, which are different from his, as being errors in the child which he must make speed to correct, there arises between the strong and the weak a struggle which is fatal to mankind. [8]

John Bradshaw, a leading expert in the adult addictive recovery movement, also speaks to the importance of children experiencing unconditional love and acceptance of self throughout their lifetime.

The unconditional love and acceptance of self seems to be the hardest task for all humankind. Refusing to accept our "real selves," we try to create more powerful fake selves or give up and become less than human. This results in a lifetime of cover-up and secrecy. This secrecy and hiding is the basic cause of suffering for all of us.

Total self-love and acceptance is the only foundation for happiness and the love of others. Without total self-love and acceptance, we are doomed to the enervative task of creating false selves. [9]

Children who grow up without supportive adults to recognize them as the beautiful people they are often experience shame, guilt, resentment, and anger. These powerful negative feelings become the seeds of violence and war. Not finding acceptance from family and other adults, they often seek solace through addictions and acceptance through involvement in violent or self-abusive activities such as street gangs, hate groups, prostitution, drugs, bullying, etc.

It is we, as adults, who reflect their self-image back to the children. We can only "see" what we know. Our own lens colors our vision. It is, therefore, our responsibility to continually clean our lens of perception, let go our shame and accept and love ourselves, so we can offer unconditional love and acceptance to the children. In an earlier book, *Shining Through—A Teacher's Handbook on Transformation*, I wrote:

As teachers, we are significant others in the children's development of self-concept. It is our responsibility to reflect the children's true nature as much as possible. Through our work toward self-perfection, we realize greater creativity, see the children in a clearer light and have greater ability to support them in the construction of their personalities and talents.[10]

To educate for lasting peace, we must begin at birth. Children come into this world with pure love or light in their hearts. When this love is recognized and consistently reflected back to them, they are able to develop their fullest potential and become responsible, peace-loving citizens of the world. However, when the significant adults in their lives fail to see them in this manner, and instead, reflect negative attributes back to them, children assume negative self images, experience deep frustration and often become unproductive or violent members of society.

The activities in this book systematically nurture this love in young children. The activities reinforce how special they are, and give them greater understanding of how their bodies, minds, and emotions can be managed so that this light of love can shine through all they do. With this knowledge, the children can more easily maintain positive self-images, make thoughtful choices, manifest respectful, cooperative behavior and develop self-management skills to stay centered in their love. What greater gifts can we give our children?

These activities were field tested in six multiage (3 through 6 years) early childhood classrooms at the Montessori School of Denver. Each week I presented the same activity to each class. The reaction of the children was heartwarming. They loved it! Many parents commented on how their children enthusiastically told them about these peace activities each week. A number of these parent comments, as well as teacher comments, are included within each activity.

The children especially relate to the concept of the love light—a simple yellow felt circle that can be pinned onto their chests whenever they wish. The love light gives them a concrete symbol to express who they are—beings filled with love and light.

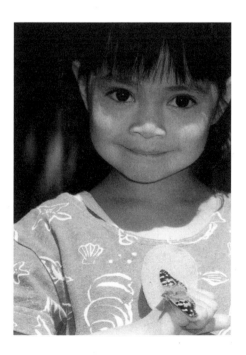

A CHILD'S VISION OF PEACE*

I am a child with a vision to share
Of a world of peace and a world of care.

I so recently came to planet earth
That I remember the peace I had at birth.

Please see my love and nurture me
To make peace on Earth a reality.

—SONNIE MCFARLAND

*This is also a song included in peace music (see page 119)

The Flower of Peace Model

To move from a culture of violence to a culture of peace, peace education must be included in every classroom at all levels of education. Following is a systematic and integrated holistic model that serves as a framework for peace education from birth through adulthood. As a holistic model, the outer world is seen as a reflection of the collective inner world of people. It is only through changing the hearts of individuals that lasting peace can be maintained. Political peace is only as good as the personal peace among the people.

The six basic elements of The Flower of Peace Model fall into one of the following categories:

- Spirit of Love
- Basic Needs and Human Rights
- Self Awareness
- Community Awareness
- Cultural Awareness
- Environmental Awareness

Central to this study is the nurturing of the Spirit of Love—the core of holistic peace education.

Spirit of Love

The word spirit does not speak to any particular culture or religion but rather the connecting love that resides deep within all people, all of nature and throughout the universe. This model focuses on the interrelationship of all things with the Spirit of Love as the common bond.

As stated earlier, peace must begin with the individual and evolve outward from the love within each person. As children become aware of and experience the deep abiding love within them, they begin to manifest it in other aspects of their lives. A new consciousness of peace grows among the children, creative ideas emerge, sharing happens more naturally, cooperation is more frequent and love is expressed more freely, and spontaneity and joy abound. This holistic framework for peace education provides the opportunity for children, as well as adults, to experience peace on a micro level that will eventually move into the macro level of world peace.

Basic Needs and Human Rights

In order for peace to flourish and basic human dignity to be sustained, people's basic needs for food, clothing, shelter, safety, health care, education, work and freedom must be met. According to Abraham Maslow's *Hierarchy of Needs* theory, we must have our basic preservation and safety needs met before we can focus on higher level needs such as belonging, love, esteem and self-actualization. Therefore, it is important to include, in our peace education study, a focus on the Basic Needs and Human Rights of all people. This will help children develop compassion, respect and understanding for all cultures and people of the world.

Self Awareness

Self Awareness activities are those that bring greater understanding and appreciation of the beauty, characteristics, talents and creative potential within each individual. By studying the relationship of body, mind, emotions and spirit, children develop a greater sense of well being and self-confidence because they learn to identify with their light of love and use it to guide their choices and actions. Some Self Awareness activities include: deep breathing, relaxation, sensory awareness, responsible choice-making, positive and negative mind, imagination, emotional recognition and expression, empathetic understanding, character education, creative expression and silence.

Community Awareness

Community Awareness activities focus on developing safe and nurturing climates, providing open group processes and communication patterns, supporting positive individual identities and fostering cooperative relationships within communities. This work encourages respect for the essential nature of others and facilitates effective interpersonal relationships, both of which are essential for peaceful living. The most significant communities include family, friends, classmates, neighbors and work and social groups. Some Community Awareness activities include: grace and courtesy, cooperative learning, communication skills, problem solving, conflict resolution, acknowledgments, community service and conscious community building.

Cultural Awareness

Cultural Awareness activities focus on recognizing the connection or commonality among people, understanding and appreciating cultures, developing compassion for others and encouraging commitment and involvement when responsible action is called for. An effective way to do this is to emphasize the similarities and fundamental needs of people and then explore the cultural differences with fascination and respect. Some Cultural Awareness activities include: fundamental needs of all humans, cultural studies and exchanges, diversity education, celebrations, service learning and study of the cultural work of the United Nations.

Environmental Awareness

Environmental Awareness activities focus on establishing an appreciation for the interconnectedness and fragility of our global environment, including our place in it. Further, it focuses on nurturing empathy and care for the environment, encouraging responsible use of the environmental resources, and promoting responsible engagement when action is called for. This work goes beyond the academic study of the elements of the environment by inspiring awe and wonder in the student. Some Environmental Awareness activities include: study of the universe, ecology, use of resources, scientific discoveries, humanitarian projects study of the environmental work of the United Nations.

The Flower of Peace Model Symbolized

Self Awareness, Community Awareness, Cultural Awareness and Environmental Awareness are represented as individual circles.

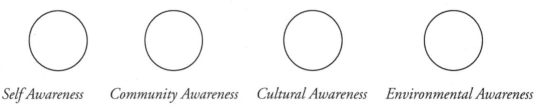

Self Awareness   *Community Awareness*   *Cultural Awareness*   *Environmental Awareness*

In our lives, self, community, cultural and environmental awareness do not stand alone. They overlap and affect one another. We can symbolize this by bringing these four circles of awareness together to form a quatrefoil. Where the circles intersect, we have the Spirit of Love. Symbolically this represents the basis of holistic peace education. For a lasting peace to be maintained, individuals must first experience inner peace, which comes from identification with the Spirit of Love within. From this center comes recognition of the Spirit of Love in community, culture and the environment.

"The Flower of Peace"

Self
Awareness

Environmental
Awareness

Spirit

Community
Awareness

Cultural
Awareness

The Four Stages of Development

In addition to the four circles of awareness, there are four basic stages of development from birth to adulthood. The four stages include:

- birth to 6
- 6 to 12
- 12 to 18
- 18 to 24 +

At each stage of development, it is important throughout the year to consciously implement activities and facilitate experiences in the areas of self, community, cultural and environmental awareness.

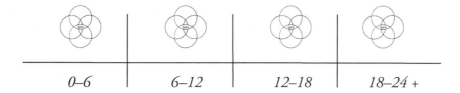

0–6	*6–12*	*12–18*	*18–24 +*

By combining the above elements, we can form a beautiful lotus flower. The green leaf pad symbolically represents the Basic Needs and Human Rights. Next, we place each of the four quatrefoils, representing peace education at all four stages of development, on top of one another. The Spirit of Love is at the center of the flower as it connects all and creates relationships of peace.

By Abra Houston

The lotus flower grows in the mud and flourishes from the nutrients of the mud. When conscious education for peace happens, level by level, a blossoming happens within the hearts of children. When we consciously implement peace education using The Flower of Peace Model, we help the spirits and potential of children bloom out of the mud and challenges of life.

The Flower of Peace Model is the framework I used as I created the activities in this book. They are designed to supplement and enhance other on-going peace activities already a part of your classroom or home environment. I strongly recommend that you take the time to analyze your present classroom or home activities to see what you are already doing in the areas of self, community, cultural and environmental awareness. This will help you know which areas are strengths and which areas need more emphasis so that you maintain balance among the four areas of awareness.

To help you, the reader, understand the focus of each activity in this book, I indicate "Self Awareness," "Community Awareness," "Cultural Awareness," and/or "Environmental Awareness" at the beginning of each activity.

The Nature of Young Children

— Montessori School of McLean © 2002

"See the peace in one another,
Feel the love between each other,
We are all sisters and brothers,
Pass it on."

from The Peace Song   Judith Darroun-Ford © 2002

Picture by permission of Nina Gibson[11]

Out of the waters of chaos emerged the lotus. When its petals opened, within was the Golden Child. Light from the child pushed back all the darkness and this is where creation came from—the light of the child." [12]

—Ancient Egyptian Creation Myth

This amazing picture and ancient myth speak clearly of the light that manifests itself so completely in the life of the young child. Children's spirits shine brightly with pure light and love when they enter this world. There is no greater purity than the guileless love of a child. Children join the human family bearing potential gifts that, if nurtured, will help "push back the darkness" and bring greater love and light to the world. This love, the essence of peace, is the children.

Maria Montessori recognized the unique nature of young children between the ages of birth and 6 and the potential gifts they bring to the world.

There is in the child a special kind of sensitivity which leads him to absorb everything about him, and it is this work of observing and absorbing that alone enables him to adapt himself to life. He does it in virtue of an unconscious power that only exists in childhood . . . If we really aspire to better things, as spreading the light of civilization more widely in a given populace, it is to the children we must turn to achieve these ends. "[13]

Young children's minds are like sponges and absorb what they see, hear, touch, smell, taste and feel from their environments. Children process this information unconsciously and create their personalities from these experiences.

This fashioning of the human personality is a secret work of "incarnation." The child is an enigma. All that we know is that he has the highest potentialities, but we do not know what he will be. He must "become incarnate" with the help of his own will. [14]

As stated above, children have an inner drive to construct themselves into their highest potentialities. Their work is to construct themselves according to their "secret" inner map. As adults it is important to respect this inner work of the children and honor their desire for independence. We must develop sensitivity to their developing interests and needs and, to the best of our ability, provide environments and experiences for them in which they can exercise independence, freedom and choice.

Although young children embody pure light and love, they are not conscious of this and depend on the significant adults in their lives to reflect their essential love back to them. Children become what is mirrored to them. If children are seen through negative eyes, they reflect negative behavior. If they are seen through eyes of love and appreciation, they reflect love and peace. Ken Carey, author of *The Third Millennium*, spoke of this when he said:

Help them to blossom into all they can be—sure of themselves, confident in the wisdom, the life that lives within them . . . When you see their beauty and perfection, when you affirm their eternal reality of being, when you see it in their eyes, you cannot help but draw it forth. [15]

As parents and teachers, we can help our children remember who they are by saying to them:

I see your love. I see it sparkle in your eyes. I see it when you smile. I bring my heart to you. I trust and respect you for who you are and who you will become. I will be with you wherever you wish to stand. You are safe and I love you.

In addition to enjoying unconditional love, children flourish in environments that nurture their love and draw them into positive engagement. Phil Wishon, Editor of the *Colorado Early Childhood Journal*, speaks to this kind of environment.

One begins to awaken children's spirits when one places the child in her rightful place in the center of the curriculum. Thus, the curriculum emerges from the child as opposed to being set in advance. The environment becomes "home"—even body—to the child. It becomes a place wherein the child is at such ease that the form and content of her deepest concerns and most heart-felt dreams are stirred to life—and allowed to flourish. [16]

Maria Montessori speaks of a need to create environments where the spirits of children are protected and nourished, thus allowing them to realize their potential.

The child becoming incarnate is a spiritual embryo which needs its own special environment. Just as a physical embryo needs its mother's womb in which to grow, so the spiritual embryo needs to be protected by an external environment that is warm with love and rich in nourishment, where everything is disposed to welcome, and nothing to harm it . . . We should regard this secret effort of the child as something sacred. We should welcome its arduous manifestations since it is in this creative period that an individual's future personality is determined.[17]

Aline D. Wolf, in her pivotal book entitled Nurturing the Spirit in Non-Sectarian Classrooms, speaks to our task of nurturing the spirit of the children.

Our task as spiritual nurturers becomes easier when we realize that we do not have to instill spirituality in a child, we have only to protect it from being trampled and to nourish its natural growth.[18]

Nourishing children's natural growth requires that we continually reflect their light of love back to them and provide peaceful environments that attract and engage them by meeting their physical, mental, emotional and spiritual needs. When this happens, children recognize their own love, express their love through positive actions, make choices based on love rather than fear and enthusiastically seek out what they need to fulfill and manifest their secret potential. When children experience environments of peace during early childhood, peace becomes an integral part of their personalities, and they are more prepared to manifest it throughout their lives. What children experience during early childhood strongly influences what they internalize and who they will become. Mahatma Gandhi once said that if we are to have real peace, it must begin with the children.

The activities in this book help children:

- Recognize and consciously manifest their love
- Make peaceful choices based on love
- Remain centered in love
- Understand the relationship of body, mind , emotions and spirit
- See the same love in other people and nature
- Interact with others and the environment in a peaceful manner

Creating Environments
to Nurture Peace

Young children have the unique ability to absorb the experiences and impressions of their surroundings and use these impressions to help form their personalities. It is, therefore, of major importance to reflect on the types of environments we prepare and offer our children. If we want them to grow up to be peaceful people, we must create environments for them that reflect peace.

Physical Environment
Children need to feel comfortable and be able to manage their physical environments with ease. To fulfill children's needs for independence, prepare the environment so they can do things as

independently as possible. If you find yourself doing something repeatedly, see if there is a way to structure the environment so the children can do it for themselves. They get much joy and satisfaction in doing things "all by themselves."

Their furniture must be the right size and weight so they can be comfortable and move it when desired. The materials and objects with which they work must be appropriate in size and allow them to be successful. Young children are in a critical period of order, so their environments need to be orderly and uncluttered. Children and nature go hand in hand so it is important to bring nature into the environment. Children are attracted to plants, animals, and flowers and are inspired to love and care for them.

When children enter an environment, what do they experience? Pay attention to the aesthetics as children enjoy art and music. Decorate the room with special art objects that you have introduced to the children. Play soft music in the background as their hearts open to music. Be aware of the smells in the room and make certain that they are pleasant. One idea is to bring in a potpourri pot. Have the children create the potpourri from the dried flowers that once provided enjoyment on the tables. Children enjoy the process of recycling the flowers into potpourri and the ritual of refreshing the potpourri pot each day.

For the activities in this book, it is important to set up a specific peace shelf for the concrete peace materials. Make the peace shelf beautiful so it will attract the children. Display the materials in an attractive manner in baskets or on trays of appropriate size. Make the peace materials available for the children to use on an individual basis. In addition to a peace shelf, it is helpful to provide a peace table or peace rug for the children to use when they resolve difficulties.

A Peace Shelf with Peace Materials

Mental Environment

When presenting thoughts and ideas to young children, it is important to make the concepts as concrete as possible. Using hands-on materials that engage the children's five senses helps children remember what they are learning. Howard Gardner, in his groundbreaking research on learning styles, identified nine separate intelligences that we use to learn:

- Verbal/Linguistic
- Visual/Spatial
- Musical/Rhythmic
- Logical/Mathematical
- Bodily/Kinesthetic
- Interpersonal
- Intrapersonal
- Naturalist
- Existential/Visionary

While we all have our preferred learning styles, we are able to access the others as well. In creating learning environments, it is important that we use as many modalities or ways of learning as possible. The more children can experience abstract concepts using these nine intelligences, the more complete their learning will be.

An example of this is to talk about a given concept (Verbal/Linguistic), see visuals of the concept (Visual Spatial), sing about it (Musical/Rhythmic), logically analyze the concept (Logical/Mathematical), touch materials related to the concept (Bodily/Kinesthetic), cooperate and interact with others regarding the concept (Interpersonal), reflect on the concept (Intrapersonal), see it reflected in nature (Naturalist), and create a vision of possibility (Existential/Visionary)

As much as possible, encourage children to make choices about their learning. When they make conscious choice about doing an activity, they are more likely to engage themselves and remember what they are learning. When children do not make thoughtful choices, it is an opportunity to intervene and help them reflect on the outcomes of their choices. It is important to do this from a supportive point of view rather than a punitive one. When we maintain a supportive attitude, the children are more likely to engage in discussion and self-reflection.

It is important to encourage the children to keep a positive mental attitude about who they are and what they are capable of doing. Help children recognize when they are experiencing fear and doubt in themselves. Help them talk it out and shift their thinking to reflect their inner strengths. This same process is helpful when children are experiencing negative feelings about others.

Emotional Environment

When children are emotionally upset, it is almost impossible for them to learn. If the amygdala gland, housed inside the brain, is negatively stimulated, it acts as a hijacker and takes away the ability of the brain to function in its thinking and reflective capacity. Children experiencing painful feelings such as loneliness, anger, sorrow and fear have a difficult time focusing their attention and minds on the task of learning. Knowing this, it is imperative that the children experience a warm, accepting and nurturing environment where they feel comfortable to express and process their feelings. The adult in the environment sets the initial tone and is responsible for maintaining this atmosphere among the children.

One of the most effective ways to keep an emotionally safe and nurturing atmosphere in the classroom is to have fun. Enjoy the children, laugh together, work together and play together. Do not take yourself or your work too seriously. The tension coming from being too serious can squeeze the love and joy right out of the environment.

To maintain a peaceful environment, there must be a process in place for children to resolve difficulties. Activity 8 Resolving Conflict Peacefully is one process that works nicely to keep the emotional climate calm and peaceful among the children. Children must learn to recognize and express their emotions as well as learn to empathize and listen to one another. Activities 17, 18 and 19 focus on these concepts. Finally, children are capable of consciously moving from one emotion to another. Activity 20 gives them some fun ways to remember some of the things they can do to move from unpleasant to pleasant emotions.

Spiritual Environment

To set up an environment that meets the spiritual needs of children is to set up an environment that provides them with opportunities to experience calmness, peace and joy. It is an environment that inspires the children to be the best they can be. Each activity in this book encourages the children to see and act from their light of love. This light is referred to as the love light.

To nurture the spiritual environment for children, look to those activities that open the heart and bring joy and happiness to the participants. Singing, dancing and celebrations are among the best ways to nurture the spirits of children.

Recognizing and affirming the light you see in each child is one of the most effective ways of creating peaceful environments. Modeling love and wearing your Love Light Pin encourages children to be conscious of and manifest their love. Making Silence every day gives children an opportunity to experience their inner light of love.

The Playful Adult

The term playful adult may seem like a contradiction when we talk about educating for peace. In my experience as a teacher, I discovered that playfulness facilitated the process of teaching and learning. When we are in a playful place, our bodies are relaxed, our minds are creative, our hearts are open and we experience joy and happiness. These very qualities bring magic into the classroom. Children love magic and will recognize the joy in your playful spirit. They will love to be in your presence.

It is in being with children that we experience the pure joy of knowing intuitively how to be and what to do for them. Earlier I talked about the need to avoid being too serious as this state creates tensions. Tension creates impatience, impatience creates harshness, harshness creates fear—the very opposite of love and peace.

Another important key to successfully working with children is to do the best we can to see them for the beautiful beings they are at their cores. Even when they are acting in ways that are not appropriate, it is important to see them as beautiful children struggling to work out human details. When we hold this attitude, our interventions with the children are much more effective because we do not create resistance through our behavior.

Holding children in the light of unconditional love is not always an easy thing to do. It takes conscious effort to clear our lenses of perception so we can clearly see the light of love in the children. When we look through lenses of anger, impatience, etc., we see only that misbehavior in others. Our actions, colored by the negative feelings, are often harsh, off target and harmful to the self-images of the children. At such times, we are out of harmony and we need to bring our bodies, minds and emotions back into balance so that our love can shine through and guide our actions. This is a continual, ongoing process for us. Our love for the children and desire to be our best for them becomes a compelling factor in our personal transformation.

How to Use This Book

When presenting the activities in this book, I strongly suggest that you come with a twinkle in your eye and your love light shining (literally wearing your Love Light Pin). Wearing the pin during the activities is a visual reminder to the children that you honor and respect their love. It is effective to wear your Love Light Pin periodically in the classroom when you feel love in your heart. This models the behavior for the children and lets them know you are aware of their love lights during the entire day.

Use drama and intrigue with the children. The use of the magic bag is great fun for the children and immediately engages their curiosity for each activity. Build a little suspense by moving slowly and deliberately before reaching into the bag to bring out the material for the day.

The children respond enthusiastically to the regular presentation of these activities. It is good to have a regular time during the week where you work specifically on these or other peace concepts. Each day, it is imperative to take advantage of the spontaneous teaching moments and refer to the ongoing peace concepts as they apply. This keeps the concepts fresh in the children's minds and helps them put the principles into daily action.

While the activities are in a chronological order, it is not necessary for you to follow this order. Suggested prerequisites are at the beginning of each activity. The activities may be modified for use at home.

Let your parents know what you are doing with these and other peace activities. Periodically, share the concepts and the exciting results you see in the classroom. If there are activities the parents can follow through at home, ask them to do so.

Most of all practice the principles in your own life so that you can sincerely communicate and model them for the children. Know that the children will enjoy and greatly benefit from these 22 peace activities. Refer to the peace concepts often, encourage the children to use the peace materials and provide follow up extension activities.

Keep the energy alive and you will experience a classroom where children want to learn, love to cooperate, help one another, and are creative. These are all the fruits of a peaceful classroom and the manifestation of the true nature of the children.

Enjoy!

1

"When she is happy, she sometimes says, 'Look, I am smiling—can you see my eyes sparkling with my love light?"
—Parent

"The children were able to tell about the work they had done which they were proud of and made their love lights shine."
—Teacher

See My Love

Focus: Self Awareness, Key Activity

Comments:
The children enthusiastically embrace the concept of the love light. It is as if they are waiting for someone to see them in their true light. Often, children come up to me smiling and blinking their eyes so I will acknowledge the fact that I see their love. When preparing for this activity, it is important to center in our love so we model what we present. It is most effective to present this activity with a minimum number of words, graceful movement, intentional silence and much love. The magic referred to in this activity implies the magic of awe and wonder. Calling the bag a magic bag adds intrigue and wonder for the children.

Objectives:
• To show children that they are special and unique
• To help children understand that they have lights of love within them
• To give them insight into how the light of love works

MATERIALS
• White or Neutral Rug
• Magic Bag
• Peaceful Person Template
• Shadow Template
• Small Picture Stand
• Flashlight

17

Preparation:
- Prior to the presentation, make the Peaceful Person Template and Shadow Template. Obtain a magic bag. (See Instructions are at the end of this activity.)
- Place the templates, the small picture stand and flashlight in the magic bag.
- Sit with the children on the floor in a circle. Carefully place the rug in front of you and hide the magic bag behind your back.

Presentation:
- Greet the children and let them know that you have something in the bag to share with them.

- Slowly bring out the magic bag, place it on the rug and tell the children that it is a magic bag with wonderful surprises inside.

- Carefully reach into the bag, bring out the picture stand and place it in the center of the rug. Next, slowly reach into the bag and bring out the Peaceful Person Template. Carefully place the template on the picture stand so it faces the children.

- Take a deep breath, pause and then calmly tell the children that this picture represents all the people on the Earth. Tell them that every person has a physical body and that each body is special and unique—some bodies are big and some bodies are small. Remind them that every person's body is different. Take time to reflect on the unique physical characteristics of the children in the classroom. For example, see how many children have brown, black, red or blonde hair; see how many children have green, blue or brown eyes, etc. Reaffirm to the children that everyone's body is different, and this makes us special.

- Pause, breathe and tell the children that inside every person is something wonderful and beautiful.

- Ask the children to close their eyes. Bring out the flashlight and Shadow Template from the magic bag. Lay the Shadow Template on the rug out of sight and place the flashlight behind the Peaceful Person Template at the center of the chest area. Turn on the flashlight and ask the children to open their eyes.

- Remain silent for a short time to give the children an opportunity to enjoy the image of light emanating from behind the body picture. Calmly tell the children that this light represents the love that lives within everyone. Explain to them that they can feel this love when they are happy, when they are loved, and when they know they have done something very well. Ask the children to close their eyes and think of something that makes them happy. After a few moments, have them open their eyes, share what makes them happy and what they feel inside when they are happy. Some of the words they might use to describe how they feel inside are: "good," "warm," "bright," and "loving." During the discussion, refer to these warm, good feelings as their love lights. Reinforce that their love lights are the center of who they are and help them to be happy and make good choices.

- Tell the children that this love light is in all people. Explain that there are times when we feel mad, sad or afraid. When this happens, it is difficult to feel our love lights. Place the Shadow Template in front of the flashlight to dim the light.

- Pause and give the children an opportunity to absorb the difference in the light. Then tell them that when we feel mad, sad or afraid, our love lights become dim but they do not go out. Ask the children to remember when they felt mad, sad or afraid. Have them reflect on how their love lights feel when they are mad, sad or afraid. At the conclusion of this discussion, reinforce to the children that their love lights are always present, but when they feel mad, sad or afraid, they are difficult to feel.

- Tell the children that when their love lights feel dim, there are ways to help them shine again. Explain that breathing deeply is one way to help their love lights become brighter. Suggest that they practice breathing slowly and deeply. Ask them to sit with straight backs and take several slow, quiet breaths through their noses. Model this breathing and slowly remove the Shadow Template from the flashlight so the love light shines brightly again. Ask the children to describe how they feel inside after breathing deeply. Remind them that when their love lights feel dim, breathing deeply will help them to shine through again.

- Review the following points with the children:

  Every person is special, unique and different.
  Every person has a love light within.
  When we feel happy and loved, our love lights shine brightly.
  When we feel sad, mad or afraid, our love lights are dim.
  We can breathe slowly and deeply to make our love lights shine brightly again.

- Let the children know that you see their love lights and you appreciate them very much. This is a good time to let them know that you see their love lights shining through the twinkles in their eyes and when they smile.

- Teach and/or sing *This Little Light of Mine.* Have the children make up verses about where they would like to shine their love. An example might be: "Shine it over the whole wide world." As you sing this song, use hand gestures.

- Share with the children that a wonderful way for them to feel their love is to make Silence. Lead them in Silence by saying, modeling and asking them to follow:

  I cross my legs,
  I place my hands on my knees,
  I make my back very straight,
  I tell my body to be still,
  I tell my mouth to be quiet,
  I take a deep breath,
  I close my eyes,
  I make Silence and feel my love.

- Tell the children to open their eyes. Acknowledge their love by bringing your hands to your heart and saying "Namaste." (East Indian Sanskrit word meaning, "I honor the light within you.") Tell the children the meaning of "Namaste:"

- Gracefully walk to the peace shelf. (See the Introduction—Creating Environments to Nurture Peace.) Show the children where you will place the Peaceful Person Template, Shadow Template and flashlight. Invite them to take it from the shelf and use it on their own.

Suggested Follow Through:
- Refer to the children's love lights often. When a child comes to you proud of what he/she has done, it is good to say "How wonderful! How does your love light feel?" This helps the child recognize the glowing feeling of happiness inside.

- Refer to your own feeling of love or the love light inside you when something brings you happiness.

- Sing *This Little Light of Mine* frequently.

- When children are struggling and their love lights are dim, encourage them to breathe slowly and deeply to help their love lights shine brightly again.

- Two good books to reinforce these concepts are: *Something Special Within* by Betts Richter and *All I See Is Part of Me* by Chara M. Curtis

Instructions for the Magic Bag:
- The magic bag should be made of cloth and be approximately 15" x 18" in size.
- Sew two cloth handles on either side of the bag.

Instructions for Making the Peaceful Person Template:
- Obtain a blue, letter-size file folder. Cut off the label tab and keep the file intact.
- Using the Peaceful Person Pattern found in Activity 20, trace the pattern onto the front of the file folder. Cut out this image of the peaceful person.
- Close the file folder and trace the Peaceful Person Pattern directly onto the back side of the file folder. Cut out this image. This forms the Peaceful Person Template.
- Cut out four 8" x 10" tissue paper sheets: two white, one orange, and one brown.
- Organize the tissue paper sheets in this order: white, orange, brown and white.
- Glue the edges of the tissue paper sheets together.
- Glue or tape the tissue paper sheets to the inside of the file folder.
- Glue the two sides of the file folder together so that the colored tissue sheets are inside of it. This forms the Peaceful Person Template.
- Protect the template by laminating or covering with clear contact paper.

Instructions for Making the Shadow Template:
- Use poster board or a file folder and cut out two 6" x 9" rectangles. Draw a 1" frame inside each rectangle and cut out the 5" x 8" opening. The result is a 6" x 9" frame.
- Cut out one 6" x 9" black tissue paper sheet and either laminate it or place it between two sheets of contact paper for protection.
- Place the black sheet of tissue paper between the two 6" x 9" frames. Tape the tissue to the inside of one frame.
- Glue the two 6" x 9" frames together so that the black tissue sheet is between the two frames.
- Protect the template by laminating or covering with clear contact paper.

2

*"When I hug or praise
Christopher, he often says,
'That makes my love light
shine!'"*
—Parent's

*"Making Silence everyday
makes a big difference in the
tone of my classroom. The
children seem much happier
and calmer."*
—Teacher

Awareness of the Love Light Through Silence

Focus: Self Awareness

Prerequisite: Activity 1

Comments:
The purpose of this activity is to give the children a beautiful Peace Candle to represent the love lights within them. It is most effective when you use this candle on a daily basis as the children make Silence and experience their love. For special occasions or celebrations, the Peace Candle adds to these experiences as well. Using this candle positively affects the atmosphere in the classroom.

Objectives:
• To introduce a Peace Candle as a symbol of the love within everyone
• To help the children recognize the feeling of love within them and name it
• To give the children an opportunity to learn to calm themselves through the practice of Silence.

MATERIALS
• White or Neutral rug
• Magic Bag
• Peace Candle
• Gift Box
• Candle Snuffer

21

Preparation:
- Select a lovely candle to symbolically represent the love and peace within each person. Wrap it beautifully as a special gift for the children.
- Place the gift box containing the Peace Candle and the candle snuffer in the magic bag.
- Sit with the children on the floor in a circle. Place the magic bag on the rug.

Presentation:
- Greet the children and let them know that you have two things in the bag to share with them.

- When you have the children's attention, dramatically take the gift box from the magic bag and place it on the rug. Respond to the children's surprise and excitement at seeing the gift. Slowly open the gift and lovingly bring out the new Peace Candle.

- Dramatically light the candle and pause to enjoy the beauty of the flame. Remind the children about their love lights. Make the connection between the lights of love that shine inside of them and the light of the candle by saying "The flame of this candle is much like the love light that shines inside of you."

- Tell the children that this Peace Candle will help them remember their love lights. Suggest that when they make Silence and are very still they can feel the warmth of their love lights. Share with them that when they make Silence the Peace Candle will be placed in the center of the circle to remind them of their beautiful love.

- Place the Peace Candle in the center of the circle and lead them in Silence as done in Activity 1. Let the Silence go as long as the children can remain concentrated (anywhere from 30 seconds or more).

- At this point, lead the children in a discussion about what they experienced during the Silence. (This discussion is to reinforce their experience and to give them a greater awareness of love lights.)

- Let the children know that you will be making Silence every day so that they can feel their love. Ask them to stand and sing: *This Little Light of Mine*.

- Reach into the magic bag and bring out the candle snuffer. Walk over to the Peace Candle and extinguish the flame. Place both the Peace Candle and candle snuffer on the peace shelf.

Suggested Follow Through:
- Use the Peace Candle and make Silence every day. This gives the children an opportunity to experience their love, and it lets them know you recognize the love within them. This can be done either at the beginning of the day or at the end of the day. When you make Silence before work time, the children often bring a deeper level of concentration and commitment to their work. At the end of the day, it becomes a time of reflection and appreciation.
- Place the Peace Candle in the same place each time the class makes Silence. It works best if it is located at the center of the circle of children. It is important for you to practice and model the joy of making Silence.
- Sing *This Little Light of Mine* frequently.
- Use the Peaceful Person Pattern (Activity 20) to make a coloring sheet for the children. Encourage them to color the body and create a love light within it.

"Alex was particularly impressed with the love light concept. When something wonderful or loving happens, she asks how bright our love lights are. When she does something for others, it makes her love light so bright that everyone has to wear sunglasses."
—PARENT

"I often hear the children refer to their love lights in discussions among themelves. They often wear their love lights in class."
—TEACHER

Everyone Has a Love Light

Focus: Self and Community Awareness

Prerequisites: Activities 1 and 2

Comments:
Having individual Love Light Pins for the children and teacher(s) to wear when they choose to do so continually reinforces, in a concrete manner, the fact that everyone has a light of love within. Knowing and honoring this in others is the first step toward nurturing mutual respect. Wear your Love Light Pin for all future peace activities.

Objectives:
• To give children a concrete symbol of their inner lights of love
• To emphasize the fact that everyone has a love light

Preparation:
• Before the presentation, make enough Love Light Pins for each child and adult in the class. (See Instructions) Place the Love Light Pins in a small basket and put the basket in the magic bag.
• Sit with the children on the floor in a circle. Place the magic bag on the rug.

MATERIALS
• White or Neutral Rug
• Magic Bag
• Felt Love Light Pins
• Basket for Love Light Pins
• Peace Candle

23

Presentation:

- Greet the children and let them know that you have something special to share with them. Ask them to close their eyes. Attach a Love Light Pin at the center of your chest.

- Ask the children to open their eyes. Do not say anything. Let them notice the Love Light Pin you are wearing. Once they see it, ask them what they think it is. Facilitate a discussion about love lights and the fact that all people have them. In the discussion point out that people sometimes feel badly and their love lights are not bright. Reinforce the idea that all people have love lights.

- At this point, tell the children that you have a surprise for them. Reach into the magic bag and bring out the basket of Love Light Pins. Dramatically show them the love lights.

- Tell them you will come around with the basket so they can receive a love light. Ask them to pin the love light on their chests. (For young children, who are unable to open and close the pin, make Love Light Necklaces by punching a hole into the felt circle and using a string of yellow yarn to create a Love Light Necklace.) At this point walk around the circle and give each child a love light from the basket. Remind the children that these are special gifts and ask them to handle them carefully. As you share the love lights, encourage the children to say "thank you."

- Once all children have their love lights on, have them stand and sing, *This Little Light of Mine*. This is a good time to let them make up a number of verses.

- Have children sit down and bring out the Peace Candle. Carefully place it in the center of the circle and lead the children in Silence as previously described.

- Let the children know that you will be gathering the love lights into a basket which will be placed on the peace shelf. Tell them that whenever they are aware of their love and want to wear a love light, they can take one from the peace shelf.

- Gather the love lights into a basket and take the basket to the peace shelf so the children see where it is placed.

Suggestions for Follow Through:

- Wear a Love Light Pin whenever you present a peace activity and at periodic times throughout the week. This action models to the children that you recognize and honor the symbol. It becomes a connection between you and the children.
- Recognize and appreciate it when children choose to wear love lights. Periodically suggest that they might want to wear love lights when they experience something loving, peaceful or when they feel especially good.
- Have a Love Light Day when everyone wears a love light. This is a good way to emphasize the love within each other.
- Create an activity in the classroom where the children can cut out yellow love lights from construction paper to take home.

Instructions for Making Love Light Pins:

- Obtain yellow or gold felt.
- Trace 2″ diameter circles on the felt.
- Cut out the 2″ diameter circles.
- Use a glue gun to attach a large-size jewelry pin to the back of each circle.

4

"I am so grateful that my daughter is being taught to value her feelings, understand nature, and respect the vital connections between all living things. This is such important work."

—PARENT

"I have seen many of the children recreating the Black Elk story in class with much enthusiasm."

—TEACHER

Black Elk's Medicine Wheel Vision of Peace

Focus: Self, Community, Cultural and Environmental Awareness

Prerequisites: Activities 1–3

Comments:
Black Elk, a holy man of the Oglala Sioux, shared his life story and vision for peace with a Nebraska poet, John Neihardt in the 1930's. In 1932 Neihardt recorded these conversations and wrote the book, *Black Elk Speaks*. This book has since become a classic text "that speaks to us with simple and compelling language about an aspect of human experience and encourages us to emphasize the best that dwells within us."[19]

MATERIALS

- White or Neutral Rug
- Magic Bag
- Table Model of Medicine Wheel
- Medicine Wheel Coloring Sheets
- Love Light Pin
- Peace Candle

Black Elk's Vision of Peace is one of the most powerful metaphors I have experienced in my life, and I encourage you to read it directly for yourself. The activity developed here is a shortened version of the original vision and covers the four objectives stated below. I consider this story an important lesson that can set a tone and atmosphere of peace in your classroom. It is a simple way to demonstrate to the children what choice is, how their choices affect their love lights and the feeling of community in the classroom. The children enjoy the story and like to create it in a concrete manner.

Objectives:
- To share Black Elk's story and vision for peace
- To reinforce the interconnectedness and importance of all life
- To introduce the concepts of the Road of Difficulties and the Road of Peace
- To introduce the symbol of the flowering tree and its connection to personal love lights

Preparation:
- Prior to the presentation create a table model of the Medicine Wheel (See Instructions) and place it on a circular tray or basket. Duplicate copies of the Medicine Wheel Coloring Sheets found at the end of this Activity and place them on a tray or basket with colored pencils, crayons or markers. Place the completed work in the magic bag.
- Sit with the children on the floor in a circle. Place the magic bag on the rug in front of you.
- Wear your Love Light Pin.

Presentation:
- Greet the children and let them know that you have a new peace activity to share with them. When they are ready, bring out the basket containing the table model of the Medicine Wheel. Let the children know that you have a special story to tell them.
- As dramatically as possible tell the following story in your own words:

Over 100 years ago, a young 9 year-old, Native American boy, named Black Elk, lived with his family and villagers on the plains of North America. At that time there were no houses, stores or cars like we have now. Instead they lived in tepees, rode horses and depended on the buffalo for their food, clothing and tepees. It was a very difficult time for Black Elk and his family because many other people wanted to have their land. These people began to destroy the Indian villages, their land and the buffalo that the Indians depended on for food, clothing and shelter. Many of Black Elk's friends and family were also killed. All of this made Black Elk very sad.

When Black Elk was 9 years old he became very ill and his people were afraid that he would not live. Fortunately, he did live and when he became an adult he shared a very important vision of peace that he had when he was so sick. Would you like to hear about it?

Black Elk felt as if he was floating and his body was being raised into the air on a cloud. As he looked down he saw a great circle or hoop. **(Place the large felt circle on the rug and carefully spread it out.)** *In this hoop he saw all of life's creations. He saw the sun, the moon, the stars, the planets, the earth, the water, the air, and the soil. He saw all of the plants and animals including the four legged, the two legged, the fish, the birds, and even the creepy crawlies. He saw that everything was good and everything was important.*

Then he looked and saw four directions:

1. *West, (**Place the black triangle at the point of West on the hoop.**)*
2. *North, (**Place the white triangle at the point of North on the hoop.**)*
3. *East, (**Place the red triangle at the point of East on the hoop.**)*
4. *South. (**Place the yellow triangle at the point of South on the hoop.**)*

*Black Elk looked at the hoop again and saw a black road running from West to East. (**Unroll the black felt road from West to East.**) He saw that this was the Road of Difficulties or life's lessons. He saw that all people sometimes walk this road. (**Move fingers along the black road from West to East.**)*

*Black Elk then saw a red road running from North to South. (**Unroll the red felt road from North to South.**) He saw that this was the Road of Peace or thoughtful action. He saw that all people sometimes walk this road. (**Move fingers along the red road from North to South.**)*

*Finally, Black Elk looked at the center of the hoop where the two roads crossed (**Point to the intersection of the two roads.**) and there he saw a sacred tree. (**Place the tree in the hoop so the bottom of the trunk is on the point where the two roads intersect.**) He saw that when the people walked the Road of Peace by taking care of themselves, others and the gifts of the Earth, the tree flowered (**Place the flowers on the leaves of the tree.**) and birds came to sing. (**Place the birds in the tree.**)*

- After completing the story, ask the children how the story is the same as the classroom. A possible opening and series of questions might be: Do we have plants in our classroom? Do we have animals in our classroom? What else? Are they all important? What happens when we take care of the plants? What happens when we care for the animals? Are they happy? What happens in our classroom when we are kind to each other? How do we feel? Do our love lights shine? Is the flowering tree like our love lights?

- After this discussion, describe the Black Road of Difficulties in a non-threatening manner. Let the children know that this road represents life's difficulties and challenges and that everyone sometimes walks this road (including adults). Give some examples and then ask the children for times when they felt challenged or had difficulties. Have them reflect on how they felt at such times. Ask directly if their love lights shone brightly or dimly during those times.

- Focus on the Road of Peace. Let the children know that this road represents peace and kindness and that everyone sometimes walks this road. Give some examples and then ask the children for times when they were kind and cared for others. Have them reflect on how they felt at such times. Ask directly if their love lights shone brightly or dimly during those times.

- End the discussion by making a connection between their love lights and the flowers on the tree. An example might be: When we are kind and peaceful, we feel our love lights shining inside. In the Black Elk story, when the people walked the Road of Peace and were kind to each other and the Earth, the tree flowered. Our love lights and the flowers of the tree are very much alike.

- Demonstrate how to thoughtfully replace the Medicine Wheel on the basket or tray.

- Remove the Medicine Wheel Coloring Sheets from the magic bag. Invite the children to color a Medicine Wheel and create their own tree on the sheet. Take the table model Medicine Wheel and Medicine Wheel Coloring Sheets to the peace shelf.

• End the activity by placing the Peace Candle in the center of the circle. Make Silence following the same routine as the weeks before. It is important to reinforce that the purpose of Silence is to give the children an opportunity to feel the beautiful love inside of them and enjoy peace.

Suggestions for Follow Through:

• Encourage the children to take out the table model Medicine Wheel and retell Black Elk's Vision of Peace.
• Make the Medicine Wheel Coloring Sheets available for their use.
• Place labels for the 4 directions on the appropriate walls of your classroom. Make the labels match the colors of the Medicine Wheel. (West—black, North—white, East—red, South—yellow) This helps the children match the appropriate colors when they work with the Medicine Wheel.
• When difficulties arise in the classroom, treat them as challenges and lessons to be learned rather than punishable offenses. Let the children know that you are there to support them in learning lessons and finding peaceful solutions.
• When you see kind deeds and peaceful behaviors in the classroom, let the children know you see and appreciate what they have done. This might be as subtle as a smile.

Instructions for Making and Displaying the Table Model Medicine Wheel:

• Cut a 9" diameter circle out of white felt.
• Cut out four felt 2" equilateral triangles: one each in black, white, red, yellow.
• Cut out two felt 9" x 1" strips: one black and one red. (If preferred, blue maybe substituted for black.)
• Cut out one tree in brown felt (pattern attached).
• Cut out the green felt leaves (pattern attached). Glue them on the tree branches.
• Cut out five or six felt flowers in your color of choice (pattern attached).
• Cut out three to four felt birds in your color of choice (pattern attached).
• Display these materials in a flat circular basket (paper plate baskets are ideal) as follows: Place white felt hoop circle flat on the basket. Have the triangles and rolled black and red roads in a small container and the flowers and birds in a second matching container. Place these on top of the white hoop circle. Place the tree on the open area of the hoop circle.

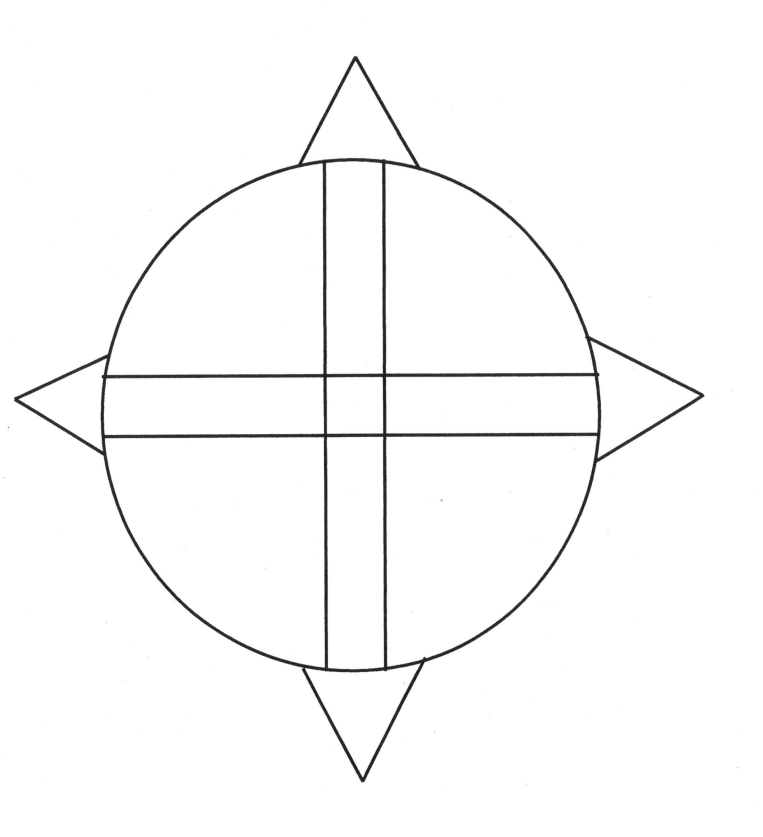

THE MEDICINE WHEEL

LEAVES

FLOWER

BIRD

TREE

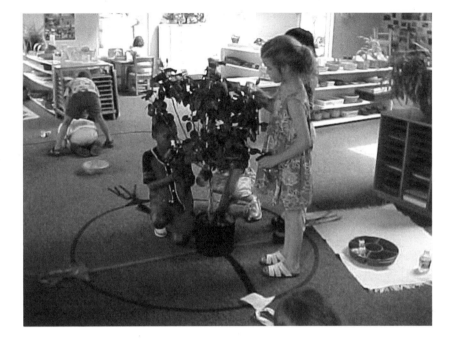

Black Elk's Vision of Peace Revisited

Focus: Self, Community, Cultural and Environmental Awareness

Prerequisites: Activities 1–4

Comments:
Once the children have heard the initial story of Black Elk's Vision of Peace and have had a chance to work with the table model Medicine Wheel, the floor model Medicine Wheel becomes a meaningful symbol of peace and harmony to them. The children take delight and comfort in bringing the Black Elk's Vision of Peace to life through this activity. You will be putting a tape circle on your floor representing the interconnectedness of all life. This circle visually reminds the children and adults of the spirit of the Medicine Wheel even when the materials are not being used. (If having the circle taped to the floor is not possible, yarn may be used to form the hoop.)

When presenting Black Elk's Vision of Peace for the second time, the story is somewhat expanded and the children are involved in the presentation.

MATERIALS

- White or Neutral Rug
- Magic Bag
- Floor Model of the Medicine Wheel
- Live Potted Tree or Plant
- Taped Circle on Floor to Represent a Hoop
- Love Light Pin
- Peace Candle

31

Objectives:
- To repeat and expand upon Black Elk's Vision of Peace
- To reinforce the concept of the interconnectedness and importance of all creation
- To reinforce the concepts of the Road of Difficulties and the Road of Peace
- To reinforce the importance of caring and nurturing in the classroom through the symbol of the flowering tree
- To give the children an opportunity to experience the Medicine Wheel directly.

Preparation:
- Tape a 3–4' diameter circle to the floor or rug. Place it in the middle of the classroom community circle to be used as the Medicine Wheel hoop. (This circle can be used for many other classroom purposes such as small group gatherings and demonstration circle.)
- Prior to the presentation create a floor model of the Medicine Wheel and place the materials in a basket. (See Instructions)
- Have a live tree or plant prepared for use as a flowering tree. The tree needs to be big enough to feel like a tree to the children (3–4' high) and yet light enough to be carried by two children. Some suggestions are hibiscus trees, fichu trees and miniature orange trees. Most importantly, the tree needs to be sturdy enough to withstand being moved and having silk flowers placed on and taken off of it. Designate a special place for it near the peace shelf if possible.
- Place the floor model Medicine Wheel and basket in the magic bag.
- Wear your Love Light Pin
- Sit with the children on the floor in a circle and place the magic bag in front of you.

Presentation:
- Greet the children and let them know that you have another activity about Black Elk's Vision of Peace. When they are ready, carefully bring out the basket containing the Medicine Wheel.

- Involve the children in a discussion of what they remember about Black Elk. The main points to reinforce are that he was a 9 year old Native American boy who was sad because his people and culture were being destroyed. He became ill and during that time had an important vision. At this point invite the children to help you tell the vision using the floor model Medicine Wheel materials in the basket.

- Following is an expanded version of Black Elk's Vision of Peace that includes suggestions for involving the children. Invite the children to pretend that they are Black Elk. Ask them to follow your actions as you begin to tell the story.

> *(Stand up slowly and raise your hands into the air as you say) Black Elk felt as if he was floating and that his body was being raised into the air on a cloud. As he emerged from the cloud, he saw a tepee with a rainbow at the open door. Through the door he saw six wise grandfathers. They motioned for him to look down. (**Look down and open your hands in front of you.**) As Black Elk looked down he saw a great hoop. In this hoop he saw all of life's creations. (**Ask the children what was in the hoop. As they respond affirm their choices and add any others not mentioned by them.**) He saw the sun, the moon, the stars, the planets, the earth, the water, the air, and the soil. He saw all of the plants and animals including the four legged, the two legged, the fish, the birds and even the creepy crawlies. He saw that everything was good and everything was important! (**Invite the children to sit down.**)*

Then the Grandfathers told Black Elk to look to the West where the thunder and lightening come from. (**Point to the West and place the black triangle at the West point of the hoop.**) *When he did, he saw 12 black horses with lightning manes and thunder in their nostrils.* (**Pick up the black ribbons representing the manes and wave them over your head as you make prancing movements to the West quadrant of the hoop. Place the black ribbon mane on the edge of the hoop at the point of West.**)

The Grandfathers told him to look to the North where the great white giant lives. (**Point to the North and place the white triangle at the North point of the hoop**). *When he did, he saw 12 white horses with nostrils roaring and manes flowing like a blizzard.* (**Pick up the white ribbons representing the manes and wave them over your head as you make prancing movements to the North quadrant of your hoop. Place the white ribbon mane on the edge of the hoop at the point of North.**)

The Grandfathers told him to look to the East where the sun always rises. (**Point to the East and place the red triangle at the East point of the hoop.**) *When he did, he saw 12 red (sorrel) horses with eyes glimmering like the stars at daybreak and manes glowing with morning light.* (**Pick up the red ribbons representing the manes and wave them over your head as you make prancing movements to the East quadrant of your hoop. Place the red ribbon mane on the edge of the hoop at the point of East.**)

The Grandfathers told him to look to the South where you are always facing. (**Point to the South and place the yellow triangle at the South point of the hoop.**) *When he did, he saw 12 yellow (buckskin) horses with manes growing like trees and grasses.* (**Pick up the yellow ribbons representing the manes and wave them over your head as you make prancing movements to the South quadrant of your hoop. Place the yellow ribbon mane on the edge of the hoop at the point of South.**)

Black Elk looked at the hoop again and he saw a black road running from West to East. (**Unroll the black felt road from West to East.**) *He saw that this was the Road of Difficulties or life's lessons. He saw that all people sometimes walk this road.* (**Slowly walk along the black road from West to East.**)

Black Elk then saw a red road running from North to South. (**Unroll the red felt road from North to South.**) *He saw that this was the Road of Peace or thoughtful action. He saw that all people sometimes walk this road.* (**Slowly walk along the red road from North to South.**)

Black Elk looked at the center of the hoop where the two roads crossed (**Stand at the intersection of the two roads.**) *and there he saw a sacred tree.* (**Bring the new live tree to the center of the hoop and place it ever so carefully where the two roads intersect.**) *He saw the people of his village living under the shade of this tree.* (**Motion with hands to show where the villages would be around the base of the tree.**) *He saw that when the people walked the Road of Difficulties and didn't take care of themselves, each other and the gifts of the Earth, the tree began to wither and die. And then he saw that when they walked the Red Road of Peace and took care of themselves, others and the gifts of the Earth, the tree flowered* (**Place the flowers on the branches of the tree or have some of the children do it.**) *and birds came to sing.* (**Place the birds in the tree.**)

- Ask the children to stand, hold hands and enjoy the Medicine Wheel. Lead them in singing: *We Are Flowers in One Garden* or other appropriate song.

- Have the children sit down. Ask them to watch you put the Medicine Wheel materials away. Let them know that the work will be on the peace shelf for them to do on their own. Show them how to carefully remove the flowers from the tree and how to carry the tree back to its designated place.

- Invite the children to join you in making Silence. Place the Peace Candle in the middle of the taped circle (where the flowering tree was). At the conclusion of Silence comment on how the feeling of love in our hearts is like the flowers on the tree.

Suggestions for Follow Through:
- This lesson provides a delightful backdrop for establishing classroom ground rules. Ask the children what a peaceful classroom would be like. Enter into a discussion and write down the children's comments. From these responses, ask for their help in creating the classroom rules. Keep the rules general, simple and sparse. Write out the rules and post them on the wall. Some examples might be:

> Speak quietly
> Walk inside
> Respect yourself
> Respect each other
> Respect the work
> Wait your turn

- Emphasize care of the plants and animals in the classroom.
- Orient the children's map work so that they lay the maps to correspond to the four directions. This helps with their kinesthetic directional awareness.

Instructions for Making and Displaying
the Floor Model Medicine Wheel:
- Tape a 3'–4' diameter circle on the floor to represent the hoop. Place it in the center of the classroom community circle. Plastic tape placed on the floor works best, but yarn will work if that is not possible.
- Cut out four felt triangles representing the four directions (one each in black, white, red and yellow. Make the triangles with two 6" sides and one 8" side.
- Create four ribbon manes (one each in black, white, red and yellow). For each mane cut two strips of ribbon about 2' long. Tie both ribbons together with a knot in the center.
- Cut out two felt roads (one black and one red) 1"–2" wide and as long as the diameter of the hoop circle. When complete, roll each road into a coil. (Some people prefer to use a blue road rather than a black road.)
- Obtain small silk flowers that can be separated into single units. If necessary add a small piece 2" green pipe cleaner to the flower to make a stem.
- Obtain a few small light-weight birds.
- Place all of these materials in a basket.
- Place the live tree in a designated place close to the peace shelf. It should be close enough to the hoop circle so the children can successfully carry it.

6

"My child speaks emotionally about the love light that is in all of us and how we need to keep it burning within us— not only to be kind to others, but how important it is to be connected to the Earth."
—PARENT

"After this lesson I observed more of the children watching each other and supporting each other throughout the work period."
—TEACHER

Good Kind Deeds Tree

Focus: Self, Community, Cultural and Environmental Awareness

Prerequisites: Activities 1–4

Comments:
This activity is an effective way to help the children focus on being kind and thoughtful in the classroom. To achieve the best results, it is important to ask the children at the end of each day what kind/thoughtful deed(s) they did or saw.

Objectives:
• To show how the love light and flowering tree symbols both represent the joy you feel when you do good kind deeds
• To inspire children to act in kind and thoughtful ways
• To recognize kind and thoughtful acts by using the concrete symbols of a tree and silk flowers
• To set a classroom tone of kindness

MATERIALS

• White or Neutral Rug
• Magic Bag
• Live Tree or Plant
• Basket of Silk Flowers
• Table Model Medicine Wheel
• Love Light Pin
• Peace Candle

37

Preparation:

- Bring in a small live tree or sturdy plant capable of holding small silk flowers. This tree must be separate from the one used for the floor model Medicine Wheel activity. The live tree for this new activity stays in one place while the tree for the Medicine Wheel is moved each time the work is used.
- Prepare a second set of flowers and place them in a basket. Flowers for the floor model Medicine Wheel activity are taken on and off the tree each time the children lay out that activity while the flowers for this new activity remain on the tree during the day.
- Select a permanent special place near the circle for the tree. Place the basket of flowers in the magic bag.
- Before the presentation, place the table model Medicine Wheel on the rug. Place the magic bag, with the basket of flowers inside, behind your back. Place the new live tree or plant in its special place near the community circle.
- Wear your Love Light Pin

Presentation:

- Greet the children. Have them stand and sing, *This Little Light of Mine.*

- Begin the lesson by calling attention to the Medicine Wheel. Engage the children in a discussion about the flowering tree. Some leading questions are: What things on the Earth are important? What happens to the tree when the people take care of themselves, each other and the plants and animals of the Earth? What happens to the tree when the people do not take care of themselves, each other and the plants and animals of the Earth?

- Discuss how their love lights feel when people are kind and thoughtful to them. Discuss how they feel when they are kind and thoughtful to others. Discuss how they feel when they take care of the plants and animals and how they think the plants and animals feel when people are kind and thoughtful to them. They will most likely say they feel good. This is a good time to refer to their love lights by asking if their love lights shine when they are involved in kind and thoughtful acts.

- Make a connection between the children's love lights shining and the tree flowering. For example, when we experience good kind deeds, our love lights shine brightly. The tree also flowers when people do good kind deeds. Our love lights and the flowering tree are very much alike.

- Involve the children in a discussion about good kind deeds. Have them name activities that are kind and thoughtful. Some ideas are:

> Be kind to each other
> Help each other
> Do thoughtful work
> Care for the animals
> Care for the plants
> Share with each other

(You may want to record the children's ideas on a large sheet of paper and post it.)

- Tell the students that you have a surprise for them. Walk over to the new tree and thoughtfully bring it to the rug. Introduce the tree to the children by telling them that this special tree will help everyone in the class remember to be thoughtful and kind to one another. Bring the basket of flowers out of the magic bag. Tell the children that whenever they do a good kind deed or see a good kind deed done by someone else, they can put a flower on the tree.

- Do a role-play in which one child does a kind deed for another child. Have the child who received the kind deed place a flower on the tree. Do a second role-play where one child successfully completes a challenging work. Have the child place a flower on the tree. Comment on how beautiful it is to see the tree start to flower because of good kind deeds in the classroom. Suggest that the tree be called The Good Kind Deeds Tree.

- Take The Good Kind Deeds Tree and basket of flowers back to their special place in the room. (It is best to have the tree and flowers next to one another and to have the tree close to the community circle so it can be easily seen.)

- Invite the children to put flowers on the tree whenever they see or experience good kind deeds. Tell them that at the end of each day, you will discuss the good kind deeds done in the class as represented by the flowers. Let them know that you will remove the flowers each day so new flowers can be placed on the tree the next day.

- Stand and sing, *We Are Flowers in One Garden* or other appropriate song.

- Carefully prepare the Medicine Wheel to go back to the Peace Shelf and ask a child to put it away. End the activity by placing the Peace Candle in the middle of the circle and making Silence.

Suggestions for Follow Through:
- During the day, when you are aware of a good kind deed, suggest that the child place a flower on the tree, if he/she has not already thought about it.
- For best results, conscientiously draw attention to The Good Kind Deeds Tree at the end of each day. Comment on how lovely the tree looks with flowers on it. Engage the children in a discussion about what good kind deeds they saw or experienced during the day. At the end of the day, return the flowers to the basket so the tree can start out empty the next day. Doing this strongly reinforces the thoughtful actions taking place in the classroom
- When you wish to acknowledge someone's kind act, place a flower on the tree and comment on it at the end of the day. By doing this you model the positive behavior for the children.
- Verbally recognize kind acts throughout the day and show appreciation.
- When you have a "good" day, refer to your classroom as a "flowering classroom." By keeping the words of the metaphor alive, you inspire the children.

7

Making Peaceful Choices

Focus: Self and Community Awareness

Prerequisites: Activities 1–5

Comments:
This activity helps the children understand the differences between the two roads of the Medicine Wheel metaphor. They learn that the black road is the Road of Difficulties, challenges and life's lessons. The red road is the Road of Peace and thoughtful action. They become aware of how they feel on each road and that they can choose which road to walk. It is important to help the children recognize what happens to their love lights when they walk each road.

Objectives:
• To help the children understand the differences between the Road of Peace and the Road of Difficulties

MATERIALS

• White or Neutral Rug
• Magic Bag
• Floor Model of Medicine Wheel
• Situation Cards
• Love Light Pin
• Peace Candle

41

- To help the children recognize which behaviors are representative of the Road of Peace and which behaviors are representative of the Road of Difficulties
- To bring about greater awareness of the consequences of walking each road
- To show the children that they have the ability to choose whether to walk the Road of Peace or the Road of Difficulties

Preparation:
- Make the Situation Cards (See Instructions) and place them in a small basket.
- Before the presentation lay out the floor model of the Medicine Wheel. Do not place the tree in the center at this time. Do place the basket of flowers for the tree on the rug.
- Place the basket of Situation Cards in the magic bag and place the bag on the rug in front of you.
- Wear your Love Light Pin

Presentation:
- Greet the children. Have them sing an appropriate song.

- Walk over to the black road on the Medicine Wheel and slowly walk along it from West to East. Ask the children to talk about what they remember about the Road of Difficulties. Once they have shared, emphasize the following points:

>   It represents the lessons we have to learn.
>   It is not a bad road even though it feels challenging and difficult.
>   All people sometimes walk this road.

- Ask the children to talk about those things that are hard or challenging for them. Some ideas are:

>   When I am fighting with a friend
>   When my work feels too hard
>   When I am angry
>   When I am sad
>   When I am afraid
>   When I am disappointed

- Ask the children to describe what happens to their love lights when they have difficulties. Remind them that their love lights may feel dim, but their love is still there. Let them know that their love lights can become brighter when they make a *choice* to walk the Road of Peace.

- Walk over to the Road of Peace on the Medicine Wheel and slowly walk along it from North to South. Ask the children to talk about what they remember about the Road of Peace. Once they have shared, emphasize the following points:

>   It represents the thoughtful actions we do.
>   When we walk this road, we feel good and peaceful.
>   All people sometimes walk this road.

- Ask the children to talk about how they feel when they are making good choices like being nice to each other, talking about their problems and doing thoughtful work.

- Ask them to describe what happens to their love lights when they are walking the Road of Peace. Remind them that when their love lights are shining, they are like the flowering tree of the Medicine Wheel. Place the flowering tree where the two roads intersect.

- Invite the children to play the Peaceful Choice Game. Remove the Situation Cards from the magic bag and lay them face down along the Road of Difficulties to look like stumbling blocks along the path. Ask a volunteer to walk the Road of Difficulties, select a card and bring it to you.

- Read the Situation Card aloud and ask the child what choice he/she wants to make. Once the child makes a choice, ask him/her to think about what would happen by making this choice. Guide the child to reflect on the consequences of his/her choice. Ask how this choice would affect the other child. Would his/her love light shine or be dim? Ask how the choice would affect his/her love light. Once the child has reflected and made a final decision, ask the other children if they think this is a peaceful choice. Engage the group of children in a discussion of why or why not it might be a peaceful choice.

- If the group agrees that the choice is a peaceful one, invite the child to change the stumbling block into a stepping stone by placing it on the Road of Peace. Next, invite the child to take a flower from the basket, walk the Road of Peace and place the flower on the tree. Verbally acknowledge the positive choice and encourage the children to clap.

- If, by chance, the choice is not a peaceful choice, engage the child in a discussion of the consequences of this choice. If possible, gently guide the child into a choice with a peaceful/positive outcome. Once the child makes a peaceful choice, follow through as before. If the child does not wish to make a peaceful choice, then he/she does not walk the Road of Peace or place a flower on the tree. You can say, "Perhaps, you will want to make a peaceful choice next time."

- Repeat this process using the remaining Situation Cards.

- Ask some of the children to help put away the Medicine Wheel. Have a child take the Medicine Wheel work and Situation Cards to the peace shelf. Invite the children to play the Peaceful Choice Game in the future.

- Place the Peace Candle in the center. Before Silence, remind the children that when they make the choice to still their bodies and make Silence, they are on the Road of Peace.

Suggestions for Follow Through:
- Refer to the Road of Peace and the Road of Difficulties on an ongoing basis.
- One teacher had success at lunch by suggesting that the class eat lunch on the Road of Peace. They talked about what that would look like, i.e. table manners, respect for each other, and using quiet voices. She reported that they had "a very peaceful lunch!"
- Read the book *We Can Get Along—A Child's Book of Choices*, by Lauren Murphy Payne, M.S.W. This book comes with a teacher's guide and some follow through activities to reinforce choice.
- Make additional Situation Cards that reflect specific situations occurring in the classroom.

Instructions for Making Situation Cards:
- Copy the Situation Cards on the following page and/or make additional cards.
- Cut out each Situation Card and glue it on gray paper cut in a shape to suggest a stone.
- Laminate the cards.
- Place the stone-shaped cards in a basket.

Situation Cards

#1

You see a child crying on the playground because she is hurt.

#4

Another child has stepped on your work and it is out of order.

#2

You are waiting in line to go outside and a child gets in front of you and pushes you backwards.

#5

You want a turn on the swing and no one shares with you.

#3

One of the children in your class calls you a bad name. You feel sad.

#6

Your best friend is playing with someone else. You feel left out.

8

Resolving Conflict Peacefully

Focus: Self and Community Awareness

Prerequisites: Activities 1–4 and 7

Comments:
This activity provides a clear procedure that helps children resolve their difficulties in a peaceful manner. During the conflict resolution process, children use a flower to signify their turns to talk. A flower is used because it symbolizes peace within the Medicine Wheel metaphor; however, a variety of objects can be substituted such as a feather or flag. Initially, it is important to act as a mediator to guide the children through this procedure. As a mediator it is imperative to stay neutral and refrain from pre-judging the situation. Nothing is ever as it seems on the surface. Once the children understand this process, step back and encourage them to do it on their own. When the occasion calls for it, redirect the process by again taking the role of mediator.

MATERIALS

- White or Neutral Rug
- Magic Bag
- Peace Flower
- Vase for Flower
- Love Light Pin
- Peace Candle

Objectives:
- To give children a simple process to resolve conflicts with one another
- To model the process for resolving difficulties using a flower

Preparation:
- Select an artificial flower to symbolize peace. Make sure that it has a stem at least 10" long. Select a vase to hold this Peace Flower.
- Put the Peace Flower in a vase and place both in the magic bag. Place the bag on the rug.
- Arrange to have two people or two children role play a common conflict in the classroom.
- Wear your Love Light Pin

Presentation:
- Greet the children. Stand and sing *This Little Light of Mine*.

- Spend a few minutes reviewing the concept of the Road of Peace and the Road of Difficulties. It is important to re-emphasize that all people sometimes walk the Road of Difficulties. When this happens, it is an opportunity to learn a more effective way to handle a situation so one can move to the Road of Peace.

- Let the children know that you have something in your magic bag that will help them when they have difficulties with one another. Dramatically bring out the vase holding the Peace Flower and set both on the rug.

- Tell the children that your two assistants (or older children) will pretend that they are having a difficulty in the classroom and are walking the Road of Difficulties. Let them know that you will help them learn a special way to resolve their conflicts so they can walk the Road of Peace.

- Have the two people act out a scenario that often happens between two children. An example might be: The first child takes a pencil from the second child. The second child retaliates by hitting the first child. The first child comes to you wanting to blame the second child for hitting and hurting him/her. Ask the first child if he/she needs your help in talking to the second child. When he/she says "yes," bring the children together and follow these steps:

Resolving Conflicts with a Flower

1. Take a deep breath, or breaths, while approaching the children. Mentally see yourself as a MEDIATOR rather than a judge.

2. Approach the children and let them know you are there to assist them in solving their difficulties. Reinforce to them that "no one is in trouble." (By saying this at the beginning, the children have less anxiety.)

3. Ask one of the children to get a rug and the other child to bring the Peace Flower to the rug.

4. Have the children sit facing one another so that they can make eye contact. It is best if you sit as the third person in the triangle. Mentally see yourself with your arms around each child so that you hold a body posture and mental framework of equality and support of each child.

5. You need to get a commitment of participation from them. Example: "It looks like you are having some difficulty here. Let us see if we can find a peaceful way to resolve this. OK?"

(Get agreement from both children.) If they are not ready to participate, have them sit out until they are ready to resolve the situation.

6. This is the time to explain the process of resolving the conflict or moving from the Road of Difficulties to the Road of Peace. At this point, explain the process. Example: "Johnny, I am going to give Susie the Peace Flower so she can tell you 1) what happened and 2) how she feels. You will then be able to tell her what you heard her say. Susie, once Johnny has heard what you said, it will be his turn to hold the Peace Flower and tell you what happened and how he feels. You will then be able to tell him what you heard him say. OK?" Get agreement from both children. By establishing the process ahead of time, the children are less likely to interrupt each other.

7. Begin the process of "I" Messages (what happened and how one feels) and Empathetic Understanding (listening). Give the Peace Flower to Susie and ask her to tell Johnny what happened and how she feels (Make sure that she talks directly to Johnny in a clear "I" Message.) When Susie has delivered her message, ask Johnny if he understood what she said. Ask him to tell her what he heard her say. If he has difficulty doing this, have Susie repeat what she said and again ask Johnny to let her know what he heard. Once he gives the feedback to Susie, ask Susie if he heard her accurately. This is her time to say "yes" or give Johnny further clarification. When Johnny does "get it," Susie gives Johnny the Peace Flower. (When Johnny hears Susie, her emotional tension begins to relax.)

8. Invite Johnny to repeat the same process (Step 7) until he feels heard.

9. When both children complete the process of describing what happened and how they feel, take the Peace Flower and place it in the vase on the rug. Sum up the difficulty, as you understand it. This helps to clarify the situation so that problem solving can begin.

10. Ask the children if the way they handled the situation in the first place was the best or most peaceful way. Usually they will recognize that it was not and that they were on the Road of Difficulties. This is the time to ask them what ideas they have to work it out in a peaceful way and move to the Road of Peace.

11. Encourage the children to come up with ideas and decide what each needs to do to make the situation better. This may include an apology, a promise to do something differently in the future and/or some form of restitution.

12. Once the conflict has been resolved, ask them if they are ready to "Declare Peace." Have them put their hands alternately on the stem of the Peace Flower and say, "We declare peace!"

13. Thank them for their willingness to participate and express confidence in their ability to make positive choices in the future.

- If time permits, act out another scenario using two different children.

- Place the Peace Flower in a special spot in the classroom and encourage the children to use it whenever they are experiencing difficulty with one another.

- Stand and sing *We Are Flowers In One Garden* or other appropriate song.

- Complete the lesson by bringing the Peace Candle to the center of the circle. Make Silence together.

Suggestions for Follow Through:

- Practice "I" messages and listening skills periodically in group settings with the children.
- Take the time to go through this process whenever two children have difficulty resolving their conflicts. While helping children resolve their difficulties through this process takes an adult's time initially, it pays off in the future. It is an activity as important as any other activity in the classroom. By taking time to help children master this process, they will be able to do it on their own in an effective manner. If we do not take the time to model conflict resolution, we end up spending more time putting out the fires resulting from ongoing conflict in the classroom.
- Encourage children to resolve their conflicts on their own once they understand the process.

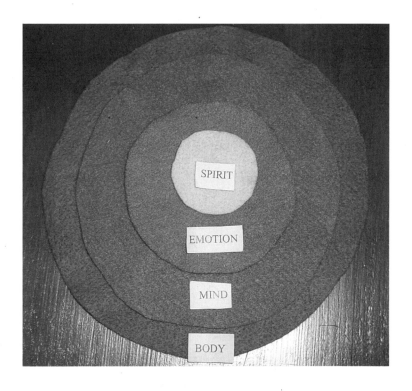

Circles of Self Awareness

Focus: Self Awareness, Key Activity

Prerequisites: Activities 1–3

Comments:
This activity is the foundation for the next twelve lessons. The Circles of Self Awareness model helps children understand the four aspects of themselves: body, mind, emotions and spirit. Through these concrete symbols, they come to understand the functions of each aspect and the impact each has on the other. As children become aware of the relationship between body, mind, emotions and spirit, they begin to understand what they can do to keep themselves in balance and harmony. When their bodies, minds and emotions are in harmony, their spirits or love lights shine through and help them make peaceful choices. This model is an important self-management tool for young children.

Preparation:
• Prior to the lesson make the Circles of Self Awareness and their corresponding labels. (See Instructions) Place the Circles of Self

MATERIALS

• White or Neutral Rug
• Magic Bag
• Circles of Self Awareness
• Labels of Body, Mind, Emotions & Spirit
• Circles of Self Awareness Coloring Sheets
• Tray & Colored Pencils
• Love Light Pin
• Peace Candle

Awareness concentrically on top of each other in a circular basket so they are all visible and the yellow Spirit Circle (love light) is in the center. Place the labels in a separate small basket. Place the basket of Self Awareness Circles and the basket of labels in the magic bag. Place the bag on the rug.

- Duplicate copies of the Circles of Self Awareness Pattern, put them on a tray with four appropriate colored pencils and place the tray behind you.
- Wear your Love Light Pin.

Presentation:

- Greet the children. Have them stand and sing *This Little Light of Mine* or other appropriate song.

- Gracefully bring the basket containing the Circles of Self Awareness out of the magic bag and hold the basket just below your Love Light Pin so the Circles of Self Awareness face the children. Give them a few seconds to look at this new material then ask the children what they think the circles represent. They will guess a variety of things such as "rainbow", "target", etc. Before long, one of the children will recognize the yellow Spirit Circle in the center as a love light. Affirm this choice with enthusiasm.

- Place the basket of circles on the rug and hold up the yellow Spirit Circle. Facilitate a discussion about their love lights. Ask them to describe how they feel when their love lights are shining. Affirm whatever descriptions they wish to share. Make a point to say their love lights inside of them are very special.

- Tell the children that another name for love light is spirit. Have them repeat the word "spirit". Show them the Spirit Label. Ask them to say the first sound they hear in the word spirit. Place the Spirit Circle near the top and middle of the rug. From the children's point of view place the Spirit Label below the Spirit Circle and say "spirit."

- Take the largest circle, representing the body, from the basket. Hold up the Body Circle and say "This circle represents our bodies." Facilitate a discussion about their bodies. Ask them to describe some of the parts of the body both inside and outside. (Include the brain, stomach, heart, bones, muscles and blood.) Let them know that their bodies are like a house for their spirit. Remind them that it is important for them to take good care of their bodies so their love lights or spirits can shine.

- Show them the Body Label. Ask them to say the first sound they hear in the word "body". Place the Body Circle at the top of the rug to your far right. Place the Body Label below the Body Circle and say "body".

- Point to the Spirit Circle and say "This represents the spirit." Point to the Body Circle and say, "This represents the body." Point to the Spirit Circle and ask the children what it represents. Point to the Body Circle and ask the children what it represents.

- Take the second largest circle, representing mind, from the basket. Hold up the Mind Circle and say "This circle represents our minds." Facilitate a discussion about the mind. Point out that the mind is different from the brain and that it helps us think, learn, make choices, imagine and concentrate. Let them know that the mind is powerful and it is important to understand how it works so our love lights can shine.

- Show them the Mind Label. Ask them to say the first sound they hear in the word "mind." Place the Mind Circle at the top of the rug to your left of the Body Circle. Place the Mind Label below the Mind Circle and say "mind."

- Point to the Mind Circle and say "What does this represent?" Repeat for the Body Circle and Spirit Circle.

- Take the remaining circle, representing emotions, from the basket. Hold up the Emotions Circle and say, "This circle represents our feelings." Facilitate a discussion about their feelings. Have them talk about the various feelings they have. Help them be aware of the fact that their feelings change frequently. Draw attention to the fact that when they feel happy their love lights shine brightly. When they feel sad, mad or angry, their love lights are dim.

- Show them the Emotions Label and tell them that another name for feelings is "emotions." Let them know that for this work the circle will be called the "Emotions Circle." Ask them to say the first sound they hear in the word "emotions." Place the Emotions Circle at the top of the rug between the Mind Circle and the Spirit Circle. Place the Emotions Label below the Emotions Circle.

- Point to each of the Circles of Self Awareness beginning with body and ask the children to tell you what each circle represents. Place all of the circles carefully back in the basket; place the labels in a separate basket.

- Introduce and demonstrate how to use the Circles of Self Awareness Coloring Sheets. Return all of the activities to the peace shelf and invite the children to use them.

- When introducing Silence today, reinforce the fact that we ask our bodies to be still, our minds to concentrate and our emotions to be calm so that we can feel our love. Bring the Peace Candle to the center of the circle and enjoy Silence!

Suggestions for Follow Through:
- Give small individual or group lessons on the Circles of Self Awareness. Mix up the circles and see if the children can label them correctly.
- When appropriate, refer to their bodies, their minds, their emotions and their spirits so that they hear the words in the context of their daily experiences.
- Make a master copy of the Circles of Self Awareness Color Sheet using the appropriate colors. Laminate it and have it available for the children.
- Make traceable patterns for the Circles of Self Awareness. Encourage the children to trace the circles onto colored paper and cut them out for their own use.
- Make a large floor model version of the four Circles of Self Awareness.

Instructions for Making the Circles of Self Awareness and Labels:
- The colors selected for the four circles have no specific meaning, with the exception of the center circle representing the spirit or love light. The Spirit Circle should be yellow or gold to correspond with the Love Light Pins. The colors I selected are:

> Body—Forest Green
> Mind—Royal Blue
> Emotions—Rose
> Spirit—Yellow

- Cut out four concentric circles in felt using the pattern on the following page.
- Place the concentric felt circles in a circular basket or tray the size of the largest circle. The baskets used to hold paper plates are ideal.
- Create color-coded labels for the words: Body, Mind, Emotions and Spirit. Place in a basket.

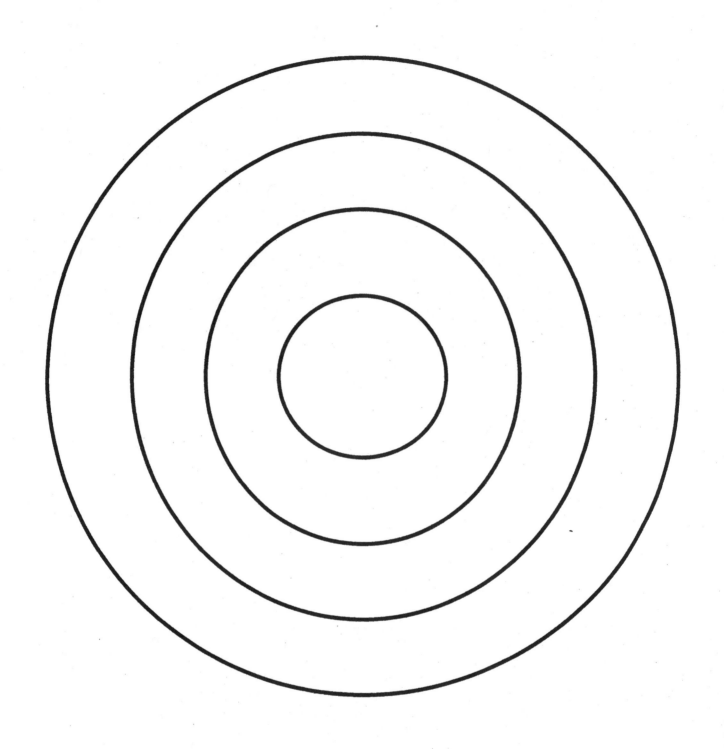

CIRCLES OF SELF AWARENESS

10

"My child often talks about his love light. When he saw his sister crying, he said, 'Michelle's love light is hiding.' He also speaks about breathing when he is angry."

—PARENT

"We practice taking deep breaths before Silence. It seems to make a difference in the children's ability to concentrate during Silence."

—TEACHER

Body
Breath Awareness

Focus: Self Awareness

Prerequisites: Activities 1–3 and 9

Comments:
This is the first of several activities on specific parts of the body: lungs, muscles, spine and nerves. The purpose of these activities is to give the children an understanding of how the lungs, muscles, spine and nerves work inside their bodies and how each affects their ability to be connected to their spirits or love lights. Deep breathing is one of the most effective ways to keep the body, mind, emotions and spirit in harmony.

Objectives:
• To give the children a visual image of their lungs
• To help the children understand how important oxygen is to their bodies
• To demonstrate the technique of breathing to full capacity (diaphragmatic breath)

MATERIALS

• White or Neutral Rug
• Magic Bag
• Circles of Self Awareness & Labels
• Human Body Book or Human Body Model
• Love Light Pin
• Peace Candle

Preparation:
- Find a book or three-dimensional model of the human body that illustrates the lungs.
- Place the book or model of the human body in the magic bag. Place the Circles of Self Awareness and their labels on the rug.
- Wear your Love Light Pin.

Presentation:
- Greet the children. Ask them to tell you what each circle represents. Hold up the Body Circle, ask the children to name it, place it on the rug and put the label underneath it. Continue in the same pattern for the mind, emotions and spirit circles and labels. Lay them on the rug left to right from the child's point of view.

- Hold up the Body Circle and say "We are going to talk about a special part of our bodies today. I'll give you a hint. See if you can guess what parts I am thinking of . . .

> They are inside of our bodies.
> They are between our waists and chins.
> They go in and out to help us breathe.
> What is it?" **(Lungs)**

- Bring out the human body book or human body model from the magic bag. Show the children a picture or model of the rib cage. Have them feel their ribs, count their ribs and become aware of how expansive they are. Let them know that the purpose of the rib cage is to protect the lungs. Show them either a picture or model of the lungs.

- Talk about the importance of the lungs and the breathing process. Emphasize the following:

> The lungs allow us to breathe by expanding (inhalation) and contracting (exhalation).
> When we inhale, oxygen enters our bodies.
> Oxygen helps us to have energy in our bodies. *(Hold up the Body Circle.)*
> Oxygen helps us think clearly in our minds *(Hold up the Mind Circle.)*
> Oxygen helps us calm our emotions *(Hold up the Emotions Circle.)*
> Oxygen helps us feel our love *(Hold up the Spirit Circle.)*
> It is good to breathe deeply and take in as much oxygen as possible.
> When we exhale, carbon dioxide leaves our bodies.
> The plants take in the carbon dioxide gas and make oxygen for us.
> Oxygen is necessary for us to live, and carbon dioxide is necessary for the plants to live.

Experiment 1:
- Have the children bend over so their lungs are semi contracted and breathe as deeply as possible.

- Have the children sit up straight so their lungs are expanded and breathe as deeply as possible.

- Compare the two experiences. Point out that when they sit up straight, they do get more oxygen in their lungs and this helps their body, *(Hold up Body Circle.)*, mind *(Hold up Mind Circle.)*, emotions *(Hold up Emotions Circle.)* and spirit *(Hold up Spirit Circle.)*.

Experiment 2:

- Lie on the floor and place your hands on your stomach and show the children that when you exhale you contract your stomach muscles, and when you inhale you expand your stomach muscles.

- Have the children lie on the floor in a similar manner placing their hands on their stomachs. Ask them to exhale their carbon dioxide by contracting their stomach muscles. Ask them to inhale oxygen by expanding their stomach muscles. Allow them to breathe deeply like this for a minute or so.

- Ask the children to stand up and sing *Head and Shoulders, Knees and Toes* or other appropriate song.

- Ask a child to return the Circles of Self Awareness and labels to the peace shelf. Show them where you keep the human body book or model for their future use.

- Bring the Peace Candle to the center. Prepare the children for Silence. Remind them that when they make their backs straight they can breathe deeper and get more oxygen. This oxygen will help them to feel their spirits or love lights during Silence.

Suggestions for Follow Through:
- When a child is emotionally upset, remind him/her to take deep breaths to calm down.
- Remind them how important it is to breathe deeply and quietly during Silence.
- While there may be other good books and/or human body models that show the lungs clearly, the one I found to be successful is: *The Human Body* by Jonathan Miller.

"My child does yoga postures at home and teaches them to our family."

—PARENT

"The children loved this activity! They get out the yoga book or cards every day. They seem eager to learn new poses and often ask what the next one will be."

—TEACHER

Body
Muscle Awareness

Focus: Self Awareness

Prerequisites: Activities 1–4, 9 and 10

Comments:
The purpose of this activity is to give the children a visual, as well as kinesthetic, awareness of the muscles in their bodies. By understanding the muscles, they become aware of when their own muscles are tense and when they are relaxed. The next step is to learn how to relax their muscles consciously. When we are relaxed, it is easier to experience our spirits or love lights than when we are tense.

Objectives:
* To give the children a visual and kinesthetic awareness of their muscles.
* To give the children a greater understanding of how their muscles work

MATERIALS
* White or Neutral Rug
* Magic Bag
* Circles of Self Awareness & Labels
* Picture of Human Body Muscle System
* Large Rubber Band
* Children's Book of Stretches or Cards
* Love Light Pin

- To give the children an experience with both tense and relaxed muscles
- To introduce them to basic stretching

Preparation:
- Find a picture of the muscle system of the body and either a children's book or cards showing various body stretches.
- Place the picture, a large rubber band and the children's book of stretches or cards in the magic bag. Bring the Circles of Self Awareness and their labels to the rug.
- Wear your Love Light Pin.

Presentation:
- Greet the children. Stand and sing *Head and Shoulders, Knees and Toes* or other appropriate song.

- Hold up each of the Circles of Self Awareness and ask the children to tell you what each represents. Place each circle left to right on the rug with the corresponding label below it.

- Hold up the Body Circle and say "We are going to talk about another special part of our bodies today. I'll give you a hint. See if you can guess what it is . . .

  > There are many of them and they cover the bones inside our bodies.
  > Sometimes they are soft and sometimes they are hard.
  > They help us move. What are they?" (Muscles)

- Bring out a picture of the muscle system of the human body and show it to the children. Tell them this is how we would look if we could see underneath our skin. Point out that the muscles cover nearly every part of our bodies. Have the children feel their muscles at different parts of their bodies.

- Demonstrate how the muscles help us move by asking the children to raise an arm or leg. Have the children make an angry face and then a happy face. Point out that their faces can change expressions because they have muscles in them. Tell the children that if we did not have muscles, we would just have to lie still because we could not move.

- Demonstrate how muscles stretch by pulling on the rubber band. Have the children hold the biceps on one of their arms. Have them stretch their arms out and then bring them up so they can experience the contraction of the muscle. Bring out the children's book of stretches or cards and show the children pictures of children doing some stretches. Lead them through a couple of simple stretches and bring their attention to how their muscles are stretching. Tell them the book and/or cards will be available on the peace shelf for their use in the future.

- Demonstrate how the muscles can be either tense or relaxed. Have another adult lay on his/her back on the floor. Ask him/her to tense his/her muscles as much as possible. Go to the feet of the person and lift up the feet about 12–18 inches off the ground. The person's body will be rigid and will lift up quite dramatically. After this demonstration, ask the person to relax his/her muscles as much as possible. Now go to the feet of the person and lift up the feet. The legs will be very limp. Gently let the legs drop to the floor. To show that the whole body is relaxed, lift up the hands and gently drop them in the same fashion. Make a comparison between what happened when the person was tense and when the person was relaxed. Ask the children if they know how the person was able to make their muscles change. (The mind sent messages to the muscles.)

Total Relaxation Exercise:

- Explain to the children that we can tell our minds to send messages to our muscles. We can ask the muscles to be tense or be relaxed. Tell them that you will lead them through an exercise so they can experience this.

- Ask the children to lie on their backs on the rug with their hands to their sides and their feet slightly apart.

- Tell the children you are going to ask them to tense the muscles of their bodies and then relax the muscles. Ask the children to close their eyes and imagine the muscles around their feet. Ask them to make those muscles very tense. Continue to move up the body asking them to tense their leg muscles, their hip muscles, their stomach muscles, their chest muscles, their shoulder muscles, their arm muscles, their hand muscles, their neck muscles and their face muscles. Ask them to "Tense, Tense, Tense" their muscles. Then tell them to relax their muscles. Repeat this one more time.

- Now tell the children you will go through the muscle groups in the same way, but this time they will relax the muscles. Proceed as before starting with the muscles of the feet. As you move up the body, ask the children to relax the muscles.

- Once you have moved to the head, ask the children to breathe deeply and enjoy the relaxation. Tell them that this is another way to make Silence and feel their love.

- Let them know that you will come around and gently touch their foreheads to excuse them to their work.

- Gently touch their foreheads as a signal that they can quietly go to their work.

- Return the materials to the peace shelf.

Suggestions for Follow Through:

- Put the book of stretches and/or cards on the peace shelf. You may want to have a special mat or rug for them to use specifically for this activity.
- Stretch as a group on a daily basis. It is very effective to stretch and then make Silence each day before excusing the children to go to their work. This practice helps them to center and tune into their inner wisdom when making choices for work. It helps them concentrate more completely on their work as well.
- Periodically work with the children on conscious tensing and relaxing of muscles by going though the Total Relaxation Exercise. This can be an effective way to help children settle down for naps or rest.
- When a child is emotionally upset, draw attention to his/her tense muscles and suggest they take deep breaths and relax their muscles.

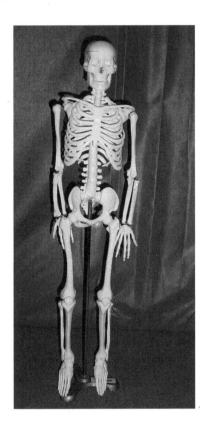

12

"I love to hear my daughter talk about peace education. It is one of the things she specifically talks about, without prompting."
—PARENT

"It was great to call attention to the specific thing that helps us sit up straight. We often talk about sitting up straight, but rarely name the spine, show or talk about it. This shows the bigger picture. 'Spine' has become a regular part of many of the children's vocabularies".
—TEACHER

Body
Spinal Column and Nerves

Focus: Self Awareness

Prerequisites: Activities 1–4, 9, 10 and 11

Comments:
This activity helps the children see the structure of the spinal column that enables us to bend and sit straight. It also helps them understand that the spinal column houses the spinal cord, which has the vital function of connecting the body and the mind through the work of the brain and nerves of the body. If possible, it is great fun to bring in a full-size skeleton for them to view and touch.

Objectives:
• To introduce the children to the structure and function of the spinal column

MATERIALS

• White or Neutral Rug
• Magic Bag
• Circles of Self Awareness & Labels
• Picture of Spinal Cord and Nerves
• Human Skeleton Model
• Vertebrae Model (optional)
• Love Light Pin
• Peace Candle

- To show the children how the brain sends messages to the body through the nerves in the spinal cord.
- To reinforce the importance of sitting up straight to breathe deeply and think clearly

Preparation:
- Place the vertebrae model and the picture of the spinal cord and nerves in the magic bag.
- Take the three dimensional human skeleton to the rug. Bring the Circles of Self Awareness and their labels to the rug.
- Wear your Love Light Pin.

Presentation:
- Greet the children. If you have a skeleton on the rug, tell the children that you will talk about a special part of the skeleton today. Have the children stand and sing *Head and Shoulders Knees and Toes* or other appropriate song.

- As described in Activity 10, hold up each of the Circles of Self Awareness separately and ask the children to tell you what each represents. As they say the appropriate name, lay each circle and label on the rug left to right.

- Hold the Body Circle and briefly mention what they have learned about the lungs and the muscles in previous activities. You can then say, "I have a new part of the body to talk about today. I will give three hints. See if you can guess what part of the body it is . . .

     This part of our bodies is at the back of us.
     It is part of our skeleton so we cannot see it.
     It helps us bend forward, backward and from side to side. *(Move your body in each direction as you say it.)* What is it? (Spinal Column)

- Show the children the spinal column on the skeleton model (or a picture if a three-dimensional model is not available). Point out that the spinal column is made of many smaller bones called vertebrae. Have them bend forward and reach back to feel their vertebrae. If you have a vertebrae model to show, bring it out of the magic bag at this time and show it around the circle.

- Demonstrate on the skeleton model how the vertebrae move back and forth to allow us to move. Ask the children to stand and bend forward, backward and from side to side. Now, have them imagine that they do not have any vertebrae so their back is one straight bone. Ask them to do their best to touch their shoes. Of course, this will be impossible. Reinforce how important their vertebrae are to their spines.

- Show the children that all of the vertebrae have holes in the middle of them. Tell them that this hole provides protection for something very important in their bodies—their spinal cords.

- Remove the picture of the spinal cord and the nerves from the magic bag. Show it to the children. Describe the spinal cord as being similar to an electric cord that is plugged into a lamp, computer or other appliance. When you plug an electric cord into the wall where electricity is stored, the electricity travels through the cord to the appliance so it can work. The spinal cord connects to the brain in a similar fashion. When the brain gets the message from the mind that it is to act, it sends this message through the nerves in the spinal cord to their respective places.

- Demonstrate how this works by asking the children to touch the tops of their heads. Once they do it, point out that their ears heard your voice; their minds paid attention and told their brains to send a message to their hands to place themselves on the top of their heads. Repeat this exercise several more times asking them to touch different parts of their bodies. Each time, repeat what happened inside their brains and spinal columns.

- Play the game *Simon Says*. Warn the children that their minds need to pay close attention to what you say so that it can stop the brain from sending the message when you do not say "Simon Says."

- Tell the children that when they sit up straight, the spinal cord works most efficiently to help them think more clearly. Remind them that it also helps them to breathe more deeply when they sit up straight.

- To end the activity, make Silence in the usual manner, but say, "Simon says, cross your legs; Simon says, put your hands on your knees, etc." This gives a little variety to the game of Silence and emphasizes the fact that their mind decides what messages are sent to the body. In other words, the children make decisions about whether or not they will instruct their bodies to make Silence.

- Return the materials to the peace shelf.

Suggestions for Follow Through:
- When making Silence re-emphasize the importance of sitting up straight so they can breathe deeply and think more clearly.
- If you notice children slumping over and having difficulty attending to their work, remind them that they will be able to think more clearly if they sit up straight.
- Expand the children's awareness of the other bones of the skeletal structure. Add materials that relate to the bones of the body.
- Sing the song *Dem Bones, Dem Bones, Dem Dry Bones.*

13

"My child learned how she could get messages through her senses to her mind. She was truly enamored with and inspired by these peace activities."

—PARENT

"The children loved this activity. The food items were such a highlight."

"They continue to use the blindfold in the sensorial work of the classroom."

—TEACHER

MATERIALS

- White or Neutral Rug
- Magic Bag
- Circles of Self Awareness & Labels
- Picture of Spinal Cord and Nerves
- Blindfold
- Five Rugs
- Three Sets of Matched Color Tablets or Equivalent
- Covered Container of Sliced Bananas
- Three Sound Objects
- Covered Container of Sliced Oranges
- Five Graded Cubes or Rings Ranging from Large to Small
- Love Light Pin
- Peace Candle

Mind
The Five Senses as Messengers

Focus: Self Awareness

Prerequisites: Activities 1–4, 9, 10, 11 and 12

Comments:
The purpose of this activity is to give the children experiences that illustrate how the five senses deliver messages to their brains and minds. By isolating each sense (sight, sound, taste, smell and touch) through individual exercises in this lesson, their awareness of how it works becomes clearer. They thoroughly enjoy this activity.

Objectives:
- To reinforce the concept of how the spinal cord and nerves work in the body
- To illustrate how the five senses deliver messages to the brain and mind

Preparation:
- Lay out five rugs in the center of the circle. Place one sensorial exercise on each rug:

> 1. **Sight**—matching color tablets or equivalent
> 2. **Taste**—covered container of banana slices (one slice for each child)
> 3. **Sound**—sound objects
> 4. **Smell**—covered container of orange slices
> 5. **Touch**—graded cubes or rings

- Place the picture of the spinal cord and nerves and the blindfold in the magic bag. Lay out the white or neutral rug in front of you and place the Circles of Self Awareness and their labels on this rug.
- Wear your Love Light Pin

Presentation:
- Greet the children. Acknowledge the work in the middle of the circle by telling the children that this activity will this help them understand how their brains get messages. Have them stand and sing *Head and Shoulders, Knees and Toes* or other appropriate song.

- Before starting on the sensorial exercises, take out the Circles of Self Awareness and review the names of each of the circles. Hold up each circle, have the children say what it represents and place the matching label on the circle. Tell the children that you will be talking about both the body *(Hold up the Body Circle)* and the mind *(Hold up the Mind Circle)*.

- Reach into the magic bag and bring out the picture of the spinal cord and nerves. Show the children the picture and emphasize how the nerves in the spinal cord go to each part of the body. Tell the children there are five ways that the brain sends messages to the spinal column and nerves.

- Ask the children if they know the five ways messages get to our brains. Lead the children in a discussion about seeing, hearing, smelling, tasting and touching. Tell the children that the name for these is the "five senses." Ask a volunteer to come to the first rug to see how our eyes, the first of our five senses, get messages to our brains.

- Select a child to sit on the rug with the matching color tablets. Mix up the color tablets, ask the child to look at each of the tablets and find its matching partner and then place them together on the rug. Allow the child to accomplish this task. When it is completed, thank him/her and ask which part of the body sent messages to the brain to help him/her know which colors matched. After the child says "My eyes," reinforce this by stating: "(child's name)'s eyes saw the colors and recognized which colors matched and sent this message to the brain. The brain then sent the message through the spinal cord to the nerves that told the hands to move and match the colors correctly. Isn't that amazing?"

- Select a second child to sit on the rug with the covered container of banana slices. This time take out the blindfold from the magic bag. Tell the child that you would like to put the blindfold over his/her eyes so that another one of the five senses can tell the brain what is in the container. After receiving permission, place the blindfold over the child's eyes. Ask the child to open his/her mouth to taste something good. Place a banana slice in the child's mouth and ask him/her what it is. After the child says, "banana," take off the blindfold so he/she can see the remaining bananas. Thank him/her and ask which part of the body sent messages to the brain so he/she knew what was there to eat. After the child says "My mouth," reinforce this by stating: "(child's name) mouth recognized that the taste was a banana and sent this message to the brain. The brain then sent the message through the spinal cord to the nerves that told the muscles to go ahead and eat it. Isn't that amazing?"

- Invite the other children to close their eyes so you can give them something to taste. Tell them not to say what it is until you ask. Give each of them a slice of banana. When all have had a taste, ask them what they tasted. When they say "banana," ask them how they knew and what part of them got the message to their brains.

- Select a third child to sit on the rug with the three sound objects. Show the children the three objects that make sounds. As you show the object, name it. Tell the child that you would like to put the blindfold over his/her eyes so that another one of the five senses can tell the brain which object is making the sound. After receiving permission, place the blindfold over the child's eyes. Pick up one of the objects and create the sound. Ask the child which object he/she heard. Once the child has identified each of the sounds, remove the blindfold. Thank him/her and ask which part of the body sent messages to the brain so he/she knew what objects were making the sounds. After the child says "My ears," reinforce this by stating.
"_____ ears recognized the sound of the objects and sent this message to the brain. The brain then sent the message through the spinal cord to the nerves that told the voice to tell us which object was making a sound. Isn't that amazing?"

- Invite the children to close their eyes and listen as you create a sound with one of the objects. Invite them to identify what they hear. Ask them how they know what object was making the sound. Ask them how their brains got the message.

- Select a fourth child to sit on the rug with the covered container of orange slices. Tell the child that you would like to put the blindfold over his/her eyes so that another one of the five senses can tell the brain what is in the container. After receiving permission, place the blindfold over the child's eyes. Open the container and hold it below the child's nose. Ask the child to tell you what he/she thinks is in the container. After the child says "orange," take off the blindfold so he/she can see the orange slices. Thank him/her and ask which part of the body sent messages to the brain so he/she knew what was in the container. After the child says "My nose," reinforce this by stating: "_____ nose recognized the smell of oranges and sent this message to the brain. The brain then sent the message through the spinal cord to the nerves that told the voice to tell us what was in the container. Isn't that amazing?"

- Select a fifth child to sit on the rug with the graded objects. Explain to the child that you would like to have him/her put the objects in a tower from the biggest to the smallest. Tell the child that you would like to put the blindfold over his/her eyes so that another one of the five senses can tell the brain how to build the tower. After receiving permission, place the blindfold over the child's eyes. Allow the child to accomplish this task. When it is completed, remove the blindfold and thank him/her. Ask which part of the body sent messages to the brain to help him/her build the tower. After the child says "My fingers (and hands)," reinforce this by stating: "_____ fingers/hands touched the objects and recognized the size of the shapes and sent the message to the brain. The brain then sent the message through the spinal cord to the nerves that told the fingers and hands how to build the tower from biggest to smallest. Isn't that amazing?"

- Review the locations of the five senses. Tell the children that the blindfold will be available for them to use as part of their ongoing work time so they can practice some of their work using the different senses to give them messages.

- End the lesson by making Silence. Remind them that their ears receive the messages to help them make Silence; therefore, it is important for them to listen carefully so the messages can go to each part of the body to make it still and quiet.

Suggestions for Follow Through:

- This is a good time to encourage new interest in the sensorial materials in the classroom by having a blindfold available to do the exercises. When you see someone do an exercise successfully (blindfolded), ask them how they knew. This will help them verbalize and better understand the process of how our five senses send messages.

- Add additional work in the classroom that uses blindfolds such as a Mystery Bag filled with objects for the children to identify by touch.

- Play *Simon Says*. Remind them that they must listen carefully and only do the actions when you say "Simon Says". Tell them you might send mixed up messages to trick them. Tell them you might tell them to do something like "Touch your toes," but if you do not say "Simon Says," their minds will have to tell them not to do it. (With this, you are beginning to give them awareness that the mind has a special function separate from the brain—it makes decisions).

- Go on nature walks and collect natural objects. Encourage the children to experience these objects and nature itself through all of the five senses. For example, smell the flowers, touch the grass, taste the berries, see the colors and hear the birds.

Instructions for Preparing Sensorial Objects:

- Three sets of matched colors—Select three contrasting colors such as the three primary colors and make two tablets of each using paper, fabric, plastic or wood. The tablet size and material should be the same so that the only variation is in the color.

- Three sound objects—Select three objects with distinct sounds such as a bell, a rattle, a triangle or a drum.

- Five graded cubes or rings ranging in size from big to small—This can be five to six cubes of clearly distinct sizes that range from big to small or a set of plastic rings used by young children to build a tower.

14

Mind
Positive and Negative Aspects

Focus: Self Awareness

Prerequisites: Activities 1–4 and 9

Comments:
This is a simple and most profound concept to share with children. It gives them the clear idea that their minds can support their strengths and recognize their spirits or love lights or it can do its best to trick them and undermine their self-confidence. Many parents comment on how much their children talk about using Positive Mind or Negative Mind. One parent said that her husband was in a grumpy mood because of a bad day at work. Her daughter told him he was being "negative" and should try to be more "positive."

Objectives:
• To introduce two aspects of the mind
• To give the children concrete symbols of Positive Mind and Negative Mind
• To help the children differentiate between Positive Mind and Negative Mind
• To empower the children to identify with their love lights or spirit as affirmed by Positive Mind

MATERIALS

• White or Neutral Rug
• Magic Bag
• Circles of Self Awareness & Labels
• Positive/Negative Mind Face on Mind Circle
• Book – *The Little Engine That Could*
• Love Light Pin
• Peace Candle

Preparation:

- On the back of the Mind Circle, make a Positive/ Negative Mind face. (See Instructions)
- Obtain *The Little Engine that Could*, by Watty Piper. I suggest this book because it is a special anniversary edition containing the original text and artwork.
- Place the book in the magic bag and the bag on the rug.
- Place the Circles of Self Awareness and labels on the rug in front of you. Make sure the Positive/Negative Mind face of the Mind Circle is face down.
- Wear your Love Light Pin.

Presentation:

- Greet the children. As in previous lessons, lay out each of the circles left to right on the rug and ask the children to name and label each circle. Keep the positive/ negative side of the Mind Circle turned over and hidden from the children's view.

- Ask the children to stand and sing *This Little Light of Mine*. At the completion of the song, ask them how they feel when their love lights are shining brightly. After this discussion, ask them to be aware of what their minds might be telling them when their love lights are shining. Some phrases you might suggest are "I am special," "I can do it," "I am a good person," etc.

- At this point, hold up the Mind Circle, keeping the Positive/Negative Mind face toward you. Say, "When our minds speak the truth about who we are, we call it 'Positive Mind'." At this point, turn the Mind Circle so the smiley face is facing the children.

- Continue to hold up the positive mind face and tell the children that sometimes our minds play tricks on us and tell us things that are not true. Some examples you might suggest are "I am not very smart," "I can't do that work, it is too hard," "I am a bad person," etc.

- At this point say, "When our minds tell us things that are not really true about us we call it 'Negative Mind'." Turn the circle 180 degrees so the frowning face is now facing the children.

- Reach into the magic bag and bring out *The Little Engine That Could* book. Tell the children you have a story to read that shows how Positive Mind and Negative Mind work.

- As you read the story, ask the children to help you by saying "Chug, chug, chug, Puff, puff, puff and Ding-dong, ding-dong" every time it comes up in the story. Practice a time or two. When the three big engines (the Shiny New Engine, Big Strong Engine and the Rusty Old Engine) come along and speak very negatively to the stalled train, hold up the Mind Circle showing Negative Mind (the frowning face). Then, when the friendly Little Blue Engine comes along and is kind, turn the Negative Mind into Positive Mind (the smiling face) on the Mind Circle.

- When the Little Blue Engine says "I think I can, I think I can, I think I can," have the children join in. Keep the Positive Mind image in front of the children until the end of the story. When the Little Blue Engine makes it to the other side of the mountain and says, "I thought I could, I thought I could, I thought I could," ask the children to join in repeating this phrase.

- Lead the children in a discussion about the story as it relates to Positive Mind and Negative Mind. Some leading questions are: Which engines showed Negative Mind? What did they think and say? Which engine showed Positive Mind? What did it think and say? Which engine was able to help the train over the mountain? Why did it work?

- Reaffirm to the children that Positive Mind will help them remember how special they are and that they are capable of doing many wonderful things. Ask them to listen to their Positive Minds as they stand and affirm their love lights. *"I am a special person filled with love!"*

- Place the book and Circles of Self Awareness material on the peace shelf.

- End the lesson by making Silence. Suggest to the children that when they become very still in Silence, Positive Mind will let them know how special they are.

Suggestions for Follow Through:
- When the "teaching moment" comes, refer to Positive Mind or Negative Mind.
- Help the children begin to reflect on what their minds are saying. For example, you might ask a hesitating child if he/she is listening to Positive Mind or Negative Mind. Ask him/her what Negative Mind is saying and then ask what Positive Mind is saying. Encourage the child to follow the suggestions from Positive Mind.
- Provide materials for the children to make a Positive/Negative Mind face on a paper plate.
- Continue to reinforce to the children that their love lights or spirits can help them decide whether to listen to Positive Mind or Negative Mind.

Instructions for Making Positive/Negative Mind Face:
- Make the Positive Mind face on one side of the Mind Circle of the Circles of Self Awareness. (The two pictures at the beginning of this activity are Positive Mind and Negative Mind.)
- Cut out two black or white felt smiles approximately 5 inches long and 1/4 inch wide.
- Glue one smile where the mouth should be and the other where the forehead would be. Make sure the two smiles at the mouth and the forehead are turning upward.
- Cut out two smaller black or white felt smiles approximately two inches long and 1/4 inch wide.
- Glue these two small smiles between the mouth and forehead placed where the eyes should be. Make sure that the eyes are in the smiling position.
- You have just made Positive Mind.
- To make Negative Mind simply turn the circle 180 degrees.

Mind
Making Positive or Negative Choices

15

Focus: Self and Community Awareness

Prerequisites: Activities 1–9 and 14

Comments:
This activity is an extension of 7 *Making Peaceful Choices* and 14 *Positive and Negative Mind.* It reinforces to the children that they make the choices for their lives and that they can make a decision whether to listen to Positive Mind or Negative Mind. In this initial presentation, two additional adults or two older children are needed to read the Positive Mind and Negative Mind Response Cards. For ongoing individual work in the classroom older children can read the cards and play the roles. The children love this activity!

Objectives:
• To reinforce the concept that children make their own choices
• To reinforce the concept that both Positive Mind and Negative Mind like to influence their choices
• To help children realize that all choices have consequences

MATERIALS

• White or Neutral Rug
• Magic Bag
• Circles of Self Awareness & Labels
• Positive Mind Mask & Negative Mind Mask
• Situation Cards Expanded
• Positive & Negative Mind Response Cards
• Love Light Pin
• Peace Candle

73

- To give a concrete experience in making choices between Positive Mind and Negative Mind
- To reinforce the concept that by making positive choices their love lights or spirits will shine

Preparation:
- Make the Situation Cards and Response Cards. (See Instructions)
- Make both a Positive Mind Mask and a Negative Mind Mask. (See Instructions)
- Place the Situation Cards, Response Cards and masks in the magic bag and lay the bag on the rug.
- Place the Circles of Self Awareness and labels on the rug.
- Before the presentation, lay out the floor model of the Medicine Wheel. Place the flowering tree in the center and put the basket of flowers on the rug in front of you.
- Select two older children (who can read) to role play Positive Mind and Negative Mind. Explain to them what you want them to do and say.
- Wear your Love Light Pin.

Presentation:
- Greet the children and sing an appropriate song.

- Hold up, name and label each of the Circles of Self Awareness. Pick up the Mind Circle, face side out, and review the differences between Positive Mind and Negative Mind. Emphasize the idea that when Positive Mind speaks, we feel good and our love lights shine brightly. When Negative Mind speaks, we do not feel so good and our love lights dim.

- Tell the children that you have a special game for them called *The Positive or Negative Choice Game*. Let them know that it is similar to the *Making Peaceful Choices Game*.

- Dramatically reach into your magic bag and pull out the Situation Cards. Walk to the Medicine Wheel and slowly walk the Road of Difficulties. Remind the children that when we have challenges or lessons to learn, we are on this road. Let them know that everyone has lessons to learn and that each time we have a challenge it is an opportunity to learn something new and, hopefully, walk the Road of Peace.

- Walk the Road of Difficulties a second time and place each of the Situation Cards face down along the path. At this point, they will look like stones on the road. Tell the children that you would like a volunteer to help with the game. Select a child and have him/her come to the Medicine Wheel with you.

- Explain to the child that he/she will walk along the Road of Difficulties and pick up a stone or stumbling block (Situation Card). Underneath the stone will be a challenge or difficulty. Tell the child that you will be sitting at your rug to help him/her read the card. Invite the child to walk the Road of Difficulties and pick up a stone (Situation Card). Return to your rug and wait for the child. When the child comes to your rug, tell him/her that you have two people who are going to help with the game.

- Invite an adult or older child (Negative Mind) to sit on your left. Ask this person what role he/she will play today. Have the person hold his/her Negative Mind Mask in front of his/her face and say, "I am Negative Mind. I will tell you what choice I think you should make." Give the Negative Response Cards to this person.

- Invite another adult or older child (Positive Mind) to sit on your right. Ask this person what role he/she will play today. Have the person hold his/her Positive Mind Mask and say, "I am Positive Mind. I will tell you what choice I think you should make." Give the Positive Response Cards to this person.

- Invite the child with the Situation Card to face the Medicine Wheel (so his/her back is to you, Positive Mind, and Negative Mind). Tell the child that you will read the Situation Card if he/she needs help and that both Negative Mind and Positive Mind will make suggestions about what to do. Tell the child that he/she will make a choice. If the choice is a peaceful choice, he/she will walk the Road of Peace and place a flower on the tree.

- Have the child sit with his/her back to you with Negative Mind sitting behind the child's left shoulder and Positive Mind sitting behind the child's right shoulder. Read, or have the child read, the Situation Card he/she selected. Invite Negative Mind to read the negative response from the Negative Response Cards. (The Response Card numbers correlate with the Situation Card numbers.) Invite Positive Mind to do the same from the Positive Response Cards. Ask the child which suggestion he/she will choose.

- If the child makes the positive choice, commend the choice and suggest he/she change the stumbling block into a stepping stone by placing it on the Road of Peace. Invite the child to take a flower from the basket, walk the Road of Peace, and place the flower on the tree.

- If the child selects the negative choice, it is a good time to ask what he/she thinks the consequences of this would be. Ask the child if this would lead to the Road of Peace or keep him/her on the Road of Difficulties. Ask if he/she would like to make the other choice so he/she can walk the Road of Peace. Most of the time, this is what happens and he/she walks the Road of Peace and places a flower on the tree. If the child does not want to make the positive choice, accept the choice and thank the child for participating.

- Repeat the game as many times as interest and time allow. Ask some of the children to help you put the Medicine Wheel materials away. Let the children know that the activity will be on the peace shelf for them to use on their own.

- Invite the children to stand and sing *We Are Flowers in One Garden* or another appropriate song.

- Make Silence emphasizing that when they are very still and thoughtful they can feel their love lights shining brightly.

Suggestions for Follow Through:
- Create an activity for the classroom in which children can make Positive Mind Masks and Negative Mind Masks.
- Continue to refer to Positive Mind and Negative Mind with the children during those precious teaching moments.
- Help children reflect on what their minds are saying.
- Encourage the children to let their love lights guide their minds to make peaceful choices.
- At appropriate times, reflect both the positive and negative consequences of their choices back to the children. When doing this, it is important to help them be more aware of what happened. It is not to make them feel guilty or shamed.
- Encourage the children to make up their own positive and negative responses.

Instructions for Making the Situation Cards and the Response Cards:
- Add four additional Situation Cards to the collection made for Activity 7. Make them to match the cards in Activity 7. Cut out each Situation Card and glue it on gray paper cut in a shape to suggest a stone. Laminate the cards and place in a basket. (Additional scenarios are at the end of this activity.)

- Copy the set of Negative Mind Responses that follow at the end of the exercise. Cut them out and glue them to 5" x 7" cards. Select a specific color for these Negative Response Cards.
- Copy the set of Positive Mind Responses that follow at the end of the exercise. Cut them out and glue them to 5" x 7" cards. Select another color for these Positive Response Cards.
- Laminate all cards.
- Place each set of cards in a separate basket

Instructions for Making the Negative and Positive Mind Masks:
- Cut out two 10" diameter circles from poster board the same color as your Mind Circle.
- Use a black marker to draw the Positive/Negative Mind face on both circles.
- Laminate both masks.
- Turn one face to be Positive Mind and the other to be Negative Mind.
- Attach a flat stick such as a tongue depressor or paint stirring stick to the back of each mask.

Situation Cards

#7

Your teacher asks you to do challenging work and you feel afraid.

#10

It is time for bed and you want to stay up.

#8

Your mother or father has made something new to eat for supper.

#9

It is a cold day outside and your parents have asked you to get your coat.

Negative Mind Responses

#1 Don't pay any attention,
you are having too much fun.

#2 That's unfair, you were in that
place first. Push him out
of the way.

#3 That is mean! Call her a bad name
back.

#4 Go and tell the teacher so he will
get in trouble.

#5 You have waited a long time.
Just go and take it away.

#6 She doesn't like you anymore.
Don't invite her to your birthday party.

#7 You probably can't do that work. It is too hard. You better put it away.

#8 Oh yucky, don't eat that.

#9 Oh, it is not so cold. Don't get your coat.

#10 Don't listen. Just keep playing.

Positive Mind Responses

#1 Look, someone is crying.
Go see if you can help.

#2 You were in that place first.
Talk to the person. Tell him how
you feel and ask for your place back.

#3 That wasn't right! See if you can talk
to her and tell her how you feel about
being called a bad name.

#4 Ask him to please straighten up
your work.

#5 You have asked for a turn several times
and no one is listening. Go and ask a
teacher to help you.

#6 She is still your best friend, and it is okay for her to play with someone else. Ask if you can play also.

#7 This work is a challenge for you and you can do it. Just say, *I think I can, I think I can, I think I can.*

#8 This is something new to eat. I wonder how it will taste.

#9 It must be cold outside. Go and get your coat.

#10 Even though you want to stay up, it is important to get sleep. Go to bed.

16

Mind

The Powers of Imagination and Concentration

Focus: Self Awareness

Prerequisites: Activities 1–3, 9 and 13–15

Comments:
This activity is designed to help children understand the power of their minds to imagine and concentrate. The more conscious they are of how to quiet their minds and focus their attention, the more successful they will be in accomplishing their tasks.

Objectives:
- To assist the children in recognizing their ability to imagine
- To give children experiences in being successful by using the power of concentration
- To offer an experience combining silence and guided imagination

MATERIALS
- White or Neutral Rug
- Circles of Self Awareness & Labels
- Classroom Work Activity
- Child-Sized Chair
- A Small Rug
- Love Light Pin
- Peace Candle

Preparation:
- Select a classroom work activity and place it on the rug in front of you.
- Place the Circles of Self Awareness and labels on the rug next to the selected classroom work activity.
- Place a child-sized chair and small rug in the center of the circle
- Wear your Love Light Pin.

Presentation:
- Greet the children. Begin holding up each of the Circles of Self Awareness. As the children name the circles, lay them on the rug and add the labels.

- Hold up the Mind Circle and review what they have learned about the five senses, positive and negative mind and making choices.

- Explain to the children that the mind also has two important powers—the power to imagine and the power to concentrate.

- Tell the children that you will do the work in front of you. Invite them to watch. Begin doing the work without imagination or concentration (look around, pay little attention) so that you are not successful completing the work. Ask the children what went wrong. They will probably tell you that you were not paying attention.

- Respond to the children's ideas of how to be more successful. Thank them for their suggestions. Tell them you will do the work again and this time you will remember to use your powers of imagination and concentration. Before beginning the work, access your power of imagination by taking a deep breath and closing your eyes to visualize yourself completing the task successfully. Open your eyes and use your power of concentration to complete the task successfully.

- Reflect on why you were successful the second time. Tell the children that first you closed your eyes and used your power of imagination to see yourself successfully doing the work. Then, you opened your eyes and used your power of concentration to remember and pay attention to your work. Because you used your power of imagination and your power to concentrate, you were successful.

- Ask a volunteer to come up and complete a task by using the power of imagination and the power of concentration. Once the child comes to you, explain what you will do. Tell him/her that you will ask him/her to close his/her eyes so he/she can use the power of imagination to see him/herself doing the task you suggest. Tell the child that when he/she is ready, he/she will be able to open his/her eyes and use the power of concentration to remember and carry out the task.

- When the child is ready, ask him/her to take a deep breath, close his/her eyes and use the power of imagination to see a picture in his/her mind of what you suggest. Slowly and clearly say the following:

    "Walk to the chair, pick it up and put it down."

- When the child is ready, ask him/her to use the power of concentration to remember how to complete the task. When the child has followed the directions, congratulate him/her. Verbally recognize that he/she used the powers of imagination and concentration to complete the task successfully.

- Repeat this process with several other children. Following are a few other task ideas:

  > "Walk carefully to the chair, sit down in the chair and stand up."
  > "Walk slowly to the rug, roll it up carefully and bring it back to me."
  > "Walk to the chair, walk around it two times and sit down in the chair."

- Tell the children that you would like to take them on an imaginary journey using their powers of concentration and imagination. Ask them to lie on their backs, take deep breaths and relax their muscles. Tell them that if they close their eyes they will be able to experience their imagination more clearly. Once they are settled, begin speaking the following in a slow, gentle voice:

  > *Imagine that you are in a very beautiful place with grass, flowers and many trees. You love it here because you can run and play and feel the sunshine warming you. (Pause)*

  > *Now imagine that you are sitting under a very large tree and a bunny comes up to you. See yourself reaching out and petting this soft, furry bunny. The bunny makes you smile all over. (Pause)*

  > *Finally you hear a voice calling to you. It is someone who loves you very much. You feel happy to hear this voice and run to meet this person. When you see this special person, you receive a warm and loving hug. Your Love Light shines so brightly. (Pause)*

  > *Imagine that your love light is growing so big that it covers the whole Earth. Send your love to all the people, plants and animals on the Earth. Imagine the whole world living peacefully together.*

Allow the children a few minutes to experience this and then ask them to slowly stretch and come back to sitting in the circle.

- When they are all sitting, begin singing *This Little Light of Mine.* For one verse sing, "Shine it over the whole wide world . . ." After the song, discuss what they experienced in their imaginary journeys. Ask them how they felt when they imagined the world living in peace.

- End the lesson by making Silence. Suggest that the children concentrate their minds and use their imaginations to see their love lights shining brightly during Silence.

Suggestions for Follow Through:
- Whenever appropriate, consciously use the words "imagination" and "concentration."
- Create activities in the classroom that require the use of the imagination such as creative storytelling and/or writing. Encourage the children to use their imaginations.
- When a child is having difficulty focusing, remind him/her of his/her mind's power of concentration.
- Guide the children in further imaginary journeys. A popular children's book with many ideas is *Taming Your Dragons—A Collection of Creative Relaxation Activities for Home and School* by Martha Belknap
- Encourage children to visualize their love lights shining brightly during Silence.

17

Emotions

Identifying and Expressing Feelings

Focus: Self Awareness

Prerequisites: Activities 1–3 and 8–16

Comments:
The purpose of this activity is to help children identify four basic emotions: happy, sad, afraid and mad. These four feelings are the most common and easily understood by children. To give this and the following lessons on emotion maximum meaning, it is important that the children have had the previous activities on body and mind awareness. For example, when the children are sensitive to the difference between relaxed and tense muscles, they can recognize tension when they are mad or afraid. When they have worked with the concept of Positive Mind and Negative Mind, they begin to recognize that Negative Mind might be contributing to their fear.

MATERIALS

- White or Neutral Rug
- Magic Bag
- Circles of Self Awareness & Labels
- Four Emotion Cards Showing Happy, Sad, Afraid and Mad Faces
- Scarf
- Love Light Pin
- Peace Candle

Objectives:
- To identify emotions of happy, sad, afraid and mad
- To help each child recognize how the emotions of happy, sad, afraid and mad affect the body, mind and spirit
- To empower the children to express their feelings

Preparation:
- Make four Emotion Cards. (See Instructions)
- Place the Circles of Self Awareness and labels on the rug.
- Place the Emotion Cards and scarf in the Magic Bag.
- Wear your Love Light Pin.

Presentation:
- Greet the children. Invite them to stand and sing *When You're Happy and You Know It.*

- Begin the lesson by holding up each Circle of Self Awareness and labeling it. As you hold up the Body Circle briefly review what they have learned about their breath, muscles and spinal column. As you hold up the Mind Circle briefly review what they have learned about the five senses, positive and negative mind, making choices and the powers of imagination and concentration.

- As you hold up the Emotions Circle remind the children that emotion is another word for feelings. Tell them that you will be talking about four emotions during this activity. Dramatically reach into the magic bag and pull out the first card. Hold it up and ask the children to identify the emotion. When they guess it, place the card on the rug in front of you. Bring out the remaining three Emotion Cards in the same manner and lay each on the rug.

- Hold up the card illustrating the emotion of "happy." Ask the children to imagine that they are happy. Invite them to look around and see how they look when they are happy.

  - Ask them what is happening to their bodies (relaxed, open, sitting up straight, breathing deeply, smile on face, eyes wide, twinkles in eyes, etc.)

  - Ask them what is happening to their minds (thinking happy thoughts, Positive Mind is saying good things, etc.)

  - Ask them what is happening to their spirits or love lights (shining brightly, feeling love, etc.)

- Hold up the card illustrating the emotion of "sad." Ask the children to imagine that they are sad. Invite them to look around and see how they look when they are sad.

  - Ask them what is happening to their bodies (frown on face, tears in eyes, slouchy body, shallow breath, etc.)

  - Ask them what is happening to their minds (thinking sad thoughts, Negative Mind might be saying things that make you feel bad, Positive Mind might be attempting to cheer you, etc.)

  - Ask them what is happening to their spirits or love lights (love light may be dim, not feeling much love inside, etc.)

- Hold up the card illustrating the emotion of "afraid." Ask the children to imagine that they are afraid. Invite them to look around and see how they look when they are afraid.

  - Ask them what is happening to their bodies (eyes wide, muscles tense, shallow breathing, arms pulled in tight, etc.)

  - Ask them what is happening to their minds (thinking about things that make you afraid, Negative Mind might be suggesting fearful things, Positive Mind might be attempting to comfort, etc.)

  - Ask them what is happening to their spirits or love lights (love light is dim, not feeling much love inside, etc.)

- Hold up the card illustrating the emotion of "mad." Ask the children to imagine that they are mad. Invite them to look around and see how they look when they are mad.

  - Ask them what is happening to their bodies (forehead wrinkled, eyes squinted, muscles tense, breathing shallow, etc.)

  - Ask them what is happening to their minds (thinking mad thoughts, Negative Mind might be suggesting mean things, Positive Mind might be attempting to have you change your negative thoughts, etc.)

  - Ask them what is happening to their spirits or love light (love light is dim, not feeling much love, etc.)

- At this point, thank the children for concentrating and using their imaginations.

- Pick up the Circles of Self Awareness one at a time and superimpose them on each other as you review what they just experienced with each of the emotions. As you talk about body, point to the Body Circle. As you talk about mind, point to the Mind Circle (use the Positive/Negative Mind side).

- When you get to the Emotions Circle and Spirit Circle, show the children that when they feel sad, afraid or mad their love light or spirit hides behind the emotions much like the sun hides behind the clouds. (Cover the Spirit Circle with the Emotions Circle) Remind them that when they feel these strong emotions of sad, afraid and mad, their love lights are still there hiding behind the emotions. Reassure the children that there are ways to let their love lights shine again and you will talk about that soon. (Place the Spirit Circle on top of the Emotions Circle.)

- End the lesson by playing the *What Am I Feeling Game*. Tell the children that you will cover your face with a scarf so they can not see what you are feeling. Tell them you will remove the scarf just far enough to allow them to see your forehead and eyes. Invite them to guess what you are feeling.

- Remove the scarf from the magic bag and cover your face. Behind the scarf make a face representing one of the four emotions. Slowly bring the scarf down so that only your eyes and forehead are visible to the children. When they have guessed the correct emotion, remove the scarf so they can see your entire facial expression. Say, "Yes, I am feeling _____."

- Let the children know that the Emotion Cards will be on the peace shelf for their use.

- Lead the children in Silence.

Suggestions for Follow Through:
- Make the Emotion Cards into three-part matching cards.
- Consciously use the terminology of happy, sad, afraid and mad when appropriate.
- Encourage awareness of others and their own body language.
- When emotionally upset, remind them to breathe deeply to calm their emotions.
- When emotionally upset, encourage them to reflect on what their minds are saying.
- When children are resolving conflict, support them in finding the words to express how they are feeling, i.e. "When you called me a name, I felt mad."
- Create opportunities for the children to say, "Right now I feel _____." A nice way to reinforce this is to have four small jars on a tray. Each jar holds a symbol of one of the four emotions, i.e. shiny beads for happy, cotton balls for sad, cut up ribbons for afraid and cut up tin foil for mad. Introduce these symbols to the children. Bring out a large jar. Pass the tray of small jars around the circle along with the large jar. As the tray reaches each child, he/she has the opportunity to say, "Right now I feel _____." At this point the child takes out the symbol of that feeling and places it in the large jar. (The core idea of this exercise comes from *A Leader's Guide to Just Because I Am—A Child's Book of Affirmation*, by Lauren Murphy Payne and Claudia Rohling.)
- Introduce new emotions to the children.

Instructions for Making Emotion Cards:
- Copy and cut out the four faces of emotion pictures found at the end of this exercise.
- Glue each face to a 5" X 7" card.
- Laminate the cards for protection
- Place the cards in a basket or tray.

Faces of Emotions

HAPPY

SAD

AFRAID

MAD

18

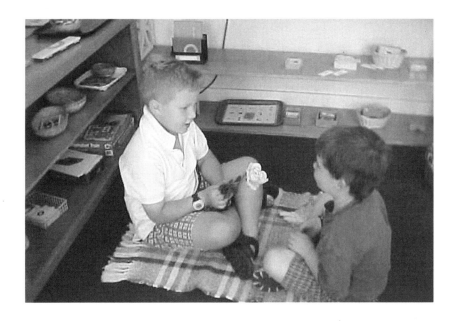

"My child had a problem in hockey with another child hitting him. He said, 'Mom, maybe he hasn't learned yet how to be peaceful.'"
—PARENT

"The children are learning to recognize physical cues in others. This helps them know what another is feeling."
—TEACHER

Emotions
Empathy Expanded

Focus: Self and Community Awareness

Prerequisites: Activities 1–3 and 8–17

Comments:
This activity gives the children an opportunity to practice the skill of recognizing the physical cues of another's emotional state. It gives them words to help communicate their awareness of and empathy for another's feelings. It also gives the child, who is expressing an emotion, words to either accept or clarify the acknowledgement of his/her feelings.

Objectives:
- To give children an opportunity to express the four basic emotional states non-verbally (happy, sad, afraid and mad)
- To give children the opportunity to observe and look for physical cues to another child's emotional state
- To give children words to express empathy for another's feelings
- To give children words to accept or clarify another's identification of their feelings

MATERIALS

- White or Neutral Rug
- Magic Bag
- Circles of Self Awareness & Labels
- Scarf
- Love Light Pin
- Peace Candle

Preparation:
- Place the Circles of Self Awareness and labels on the rug.
- Place the scarf in the magic bag.
- Wear your Love Light Pin.

Presentation:
- Greet the children. Invite them to stand and sing, *When You're Happy and You Know It.*

- Hold up each Circle of Self Awareness, ask the children what the circle represents and then lay each circle on the rug with its appropriate label.

- Hold up the Emotions Circle and tell the children that they will be playing the *What Am I Feeling Game* with each other.

- Invite two children to come to the rug and sit facing one another. Take out the scarf from the magic bag.

- Explain to the children that one child will put the scarf in front of his/her face and will imagine one of the four emotions of happy, sad, afraid or mad. When he/she is ready, he/she will lower the scarf so that the eyes and forehead are visible.

- The second child will then observe the child's facial expression and say, "It looks like you are feeling _____." If this is correct, the first child will respond, "Yes, I am feeling _____."

- However, if this is not correct, the second child will respond, "No, I am not feeling _____." If this is the case, the second child will observe again and say, "It looks like you are feeling _____." This continues until the second child correctly identifies the feeling.

- Repeat this process giving every interested child an opportunity to take part in this game.

- An extension of this game is to have the children imagine a feeling and assume the posture without using the scarf. This way the focus of observation is not limited to the eyes and forehead, but the entire body.

- Invite the children to play this game during their work time. Return the materials to the peace shelf.

- End the lesson by making Silence.

Suggestions for Follow Through:
- Encourage children to play the game as part of the ongoing work of the classroom.
- When assisting children in conflict resolution, encourage them to observe the other child to see if they can tell how he/she may be feeling.
- Talk about the word "empathy". Help the children identify times when they felt happy, sad, afraid or mad. Reinforce that all people sometimes have these feelings.

 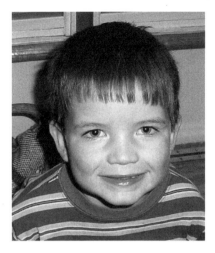

19

"My child talked to me about our love lights frequently. She drew pictures of love lights and told me that her love light was feeling weaker as a way of expressing sadness."

—PARENT

"I have observed some of the children using their breath to calm down."

—TEACHER

Emotions
Changing Feelings

Focus: Self Awareness

Prerequisites: Activities 1–3 and 8–18

Comments:
This activity is a direct extension of Activity 17—*Identifying and Expressing Feelings*. In this activity children become more aware of what happens to their bodies, minds and spirits when they feel happy, sad, afraid or mad. From this awareness, they learn three ways to change the feelings of sad, afraid and mad to a more positive state of calm. They "just enjoy" being happy. Depending on the time, it may be good to divide this activity into two or more presentations.

Objectives:
- To reinforce the children's awareness of the four basic emotions of happy, sad, afraid and mad
- To deepen their awareness of how each emotion affects their bodies, minds and spirits
- To become aware of activities they can use to calm themselves when upset
- To reinforce the fun of just enjoying being happy.

MATERIALS
- White or Neutral Rug
- Magic Bag
- Circles of Self Awareness & Labels
- Four Emotion Cards
- Four 9" x 12" Emotional Change Posters
- Love Light Pin
- Peace Candle

Preparation:
- Make the four Emotional Change Posters. (See Instructions)
- Place the Emotion Cards, and Emotional Change Posters in the magic bag.
- Place the Circles of Self Awareness and labels on the rug.
- Wear your Love Light Pin.

Presentation:
- Greet the children. Invite them to stand and sing. *When You're Happy and You Know It.*

- Hold up each Circle of Self Awareness, ask the children what the circle represents, and then lay each circle on the rug with its appropriate label. Hold up the Emotions Circle and tell the children you will be talking more about the four emotions of happy, sad, afraid and angry. As you say each emotion pull out the corresponding Emotion Card from the magic bag, hold it up and lay it on the rug.

- Follow this pattern for each of the four emotions:

  - Ask the children to show you "happy." As they do, say, "I can see that you are feeling happy. All people sometimes feel happy."

  - Ask the children to show you "sad." As they do, say, "I can see that you are feeling sad. All people sometimes feel sad."

  - Ask the children to show you "afraid," As they do, say, "I can see that you are feeling afraid. All people sometimes feel afraid."

  - Ask the children to show you "mad," As they do, say, "I can see that you are feeling mad. All people sometimes feel mad."

- Tell the children that when we feel happy it feels good and we probably want to stay happy. When we feel sad, afraid or mad we might want to change these feelings because they can be uncomfortable. Let them know that you will show them some ways they can change their feelings of sad, afraid and mad.

- Hold up the card illustrating "sad" and ask the children to show you "sad" one more time. Ask them to be aware of what being sad is like for them.

  - Hold up the Body Circle and ask them what their bodies are like. (frown on faces, muscles limp, bodies bent over, tears in eyes, hard to breathe) Tell them that one way to help their bodies when they are sad is to sit up straight and take deep breaths because it will help their love lights shine and help them think more clearly. Have them practice.

  - Ask them to continue imagining that they are sad. Hold up the Mind Circle and ask them if Positive Mind or Negative Mind is speaking? Let them know that sometimes it helps them listen to Positive Mind when they talk to a friend about their feelings. Have them pretend they are talking to a friend.

  - Ask them to continue imagining that they are sad. Hold up the Mind Circle. Suggest that another way to help their love lights or spirits shine through again is to think of something nice. This helps them remember how special they are. Have them practice this.

- Hold up the Spirit Circle and ask them what happens to their spirits when they are feeling sad. Pick up the Emotion Circle and illustrate how the emotions can cover the love light when they are sad. Reinforce that when they 1) take deep breaths, 2) talk to a friend, and 3) think of something nice, it helps their love light or spirits to shine again. Place the Spirit Circle on top of the Emotion Circle.

- Bring out the Emotional Change Poster for Sad and teach them to sing the song *When You're Sad and You Know It.* It is sung to the same tune as *When You're Happy and You Know It.*

(Depending on the time, you may want to skip directly to the emotion of "happy" and save the emotions of "afraid" and "mad" for another time.)

- Hold up the card illustrating "afraid" and ask the children to show you "afraid" one more time. Ask them to be aware of what being afraid is like for them.

  - Hold up the Body Circle and ask them what their bodies are like. (muscles tense, eyes wide, mouths tight, hard to breath) Tell them that one way to help their bodies when they are afraid is to sit up straight and take deep breaths because it will help their love lights shine and help them think more clearly. Have them practice.

  - Continue to hold up the Body Circle and tell them that another way to help them feel better when they are afraid is to relax their muscles. Have them practice.

  - Ask them to continue imagining that they are afraid. Hold up the Mind Circle and ask them if Positive Mind or Negative Mind is talking. Tell them that when they are afraid, it often helps if they think of something nice. Have them practice.

  - Hold up the Spirit Circle and ask them what happens to their spirits when they are feeling afraid (the love light feels dim). Illustrate how the emotions can cover the love light when they are afraid. Reinforce that when they 1) take deep breaths, 2) relax their muscles, and 3) think of something nice, it helps their love lights to shine again.

  - Bring out the Emotional Change Poster for Afraid and teach them to sing the song, *When You're Afraid and You Know It.*

- Hold up the card illustrating "mad" and ask the children to show you "mad" one more time. Ask them to be aware of what being mad is like for them.

  - Hold up the Body Circle and ask them what their bodies are like (tense muscles, eyes thin, bodies shaking, shallow breaths). Tell them that one way to help their bodies when they are mad is to sit up straight and take deep breaths because it will help their love lights shine and help them think more clearly. Have them practice.

  - Continue holding up the Body Circle and tell them that another way to help them feel better when feeling mad is to relax their muscles. Have them practice.

  - Ask them to continue imagining that they are mad. Hold up the Mind Circle and ask them if Positive Mind or Negative Mind is talking. Tell them that when they are mad, it often helps if they talk it out. Have them pretend to talk to someone using the Peace Flower. (See Activity 8)

- Hold up the Spirit Circle and ask them what happens to their love lights or spirits when they are feeling mad (the love light feels dim). Illustrate how the emotions can cover the love light when they are mad. Reinforce that when they 1) take deep breaths, 2) relax their muscles and 3) talk it out, it helps their love lights to shine again.

- Bring out the Emotional Change Poster for Mad and teach them to sing the song *When You're Mad and You Know It.*

- Hold up the card illustrating "happy" and ask the children to show you "happy" one more time. Ask them to be aware of what being happy is like for them.

  - Hold up the Body Circle and ask them what their bodies are like (muscles relaxed, mouth smiling, bodies open, breathing deeply).

  - Hold up the Mind Circle and ask them if Positive Mind or Negative Mind is speaking.

  - Hold up the Spirit Circle and ask them what happens to their spirits or love lights when they are happy (the love lights shine brightly).

  - At this point, ask the children if they enjoy feeling happy. Tell them you have a song about what to do when you feel happy.

  - Bring out the Emotional Change Poster for Happy and teach them to sing the song *When You're Happy and You Know It—Just Enjoy.*

- Explain to the children that the Emotional Change Posters will be available for them to help them remember what to do when they are feeling sad, afraid or mad.

- Return the materials to the peace shelf.

- End the lesson by making Silence. Ask them to "just enjoy" how they feel when they are making Silence.

Suggestions for Follow Through:
- Continue to use the terminology of happy, sad, afraid and mad when appropriate.
- When a child is feeling sad, afraid or mad refer to the relevant Emotional Change Poster and as the child to think about what he/she might do to feel better. Coach the child through the process bringing attention to the body, mind and spirit as you do. For example: "The muscles of your body seem tense. What can you do to relax them?"

Instructions for Making Emotional Change Posters:
- Copy the four Emotional Change Poster patterns on the following pages.
- Mount the individual posters to sturdy colored sheets of 9" x 12" paper.
- Laminate for protection

Words to the Songs:
The words to each of the songs highlighted in this Activity are found on the Emotional Change Posters. They are sung to the tune of *When You're Happy and You Know It.*

WHEN YOU'RE SAD AND YOU KNOW IT

Take deep breaths

Talk to a friend

Think of something nice

WHEN YOU'RE AFRAID AND YOU KNOW IT

Take deep breaths

Relax your muscles

Think of something nice

WHEN YOU'RE MAD AND YOU KNOW IT

Take deep breaths

Relax your muscles

Talk it out

WHEN YOU'RE HAPPY AND YOU KNOW IT

Clap your hands

Tap your knees

Just enjoy!

20

Spirit
Appreciating Differences in People

MATERIALS

- Two White or Neutral Rugs
- Magic Bag
- Circles of Self Awareness & Labels
- Earth Globe
- Felt Peaceful People
- Bell
- Materials for Peaceful People Follow-up Work
- Love Light Pin
- Peace Candle

Focus: Self, Community and Cultural Awareness

Prerequisites: Activities 1–3 and 9

Comments:
Children love this activity and embrace the fact that all people, regardless of differences, have a love light or spirit inside of them. This knowledge is a comfort to the children, reinforces their natural love, and helps them see the essential nature of people. At this age, children accept and celebrate differences. It is important to reinforce this view so that it remains with them throughout life.

Objectives:
- To reinforce the concept that all people, regardless of differences, have a spirit or love light
- To give the children a story to illustrate how fear can divide and alienate people while love unites them

Preparation:

- Make six felt Peaceful People who each have a different shade of skin. Place them in a basket. (See Instructions)
- Prepare the Peaceful People follow up work and place it on a tray. (See Instructions)
- Place one rug in the center of the circle with the Earth globe in the center. Place the second rug in front of you.
- Put the Circles of Self Awareness and the bell on the rug in front of you. Place the basket of Peaceful People in the magic bag. Have the Peaceful People follow-up work nearby.
- Wear your Love Light Pin.

Presentation:

- Greet the children and have them stand and sing *This Little Light of Mine*

- Hold up the Circles of Self Awareness and ask the children what each circle represents. Lay each circle on the rug with its appropriate label. Hold up the Spirit Circle and tell the children that you will be talking about how everyone has a love light or spirit inside of them.

- Carefully reach into the magic bag and bring out the basket of felt Peaceful People. Tell the children that you have a special story to tell them.

  (Holding the basket of Peaceful People, stand up and slowly walk to the Earth globe). Once upon a time, when the first people were on earth, the people were aware of all their wonderful love lights and enjoyed one another and all their many differences.

  (Hold up the first felt person. As you pick up the felt person, use the corresponding color name. For example: tan, beige, peach, cocoa, etc.) There were those who had skin the color of _____. (Place the felt person on the rug with feet facing the globe and the love light showing.)

  (Continue to hold up each felt person and repeat the above phrase. When finished, all six multi- colored felt people will be surrounding the Earth globe with their love lights shining.)

  For a long time the people enjoyed one another. They played and worked together and cared for each other and the Earth. Over time, however, people became afraid to trust people who were different from them. The people gradually forgot about their love lights and began to live only near those people who looked the same as they looked. (Pick up one of the felt people, hold it in a standing position and turn it so the love light is not visible to the children and say . . .) "I do not like how you look. I look better than you do. I am better than you are. All the people who look like me will live by ourselves and we will not share with you." (Place this felt person face down so the love light does not show.)

  (Repeat this process until all of the felt people are face down so the love lights do not show.)

  Soon all the people were only thinking about themselves. They became selfish and greedy. The people did not care about each other. Sometimes they even fought with one another. (Ask the children to close their eyes to imagine how that might have felt. While their eyes are closed, take the bell out of the magic bag and bring it to the center rug.)

*One day the people of the Earth heard something beautiful. (**Ring the bell.**) This sound reminded them to look up. They looked up into the sky and saw a rainbow made of many colors. It was so beautiful that the people began to feel something warm inside of them. It was love.*

*(**Stand up the first felt person so the love light is facing out. While holding this felt person say**) "I feel love in my heart again. Why do I need to be afraid of other people who are different from me? I will go over and apologize for being so selfish." (**Take the first felt person to the second felt person in the circle and say**) "Hello, I am sorry for treating you so badly. I would like to be friends again."*

*(**Dramatically turn the second felt person over so the love light is facing out. Speak for the second felt person by saying**) "Oh yes! I would like to be your friend again. It has been very lonely. Let's go talk to the person over there."*

*(**Holding both felt people move them to the third felt person and repeat the previous offer to be friends. Have the third felt person respond as the second person did. By now, you will have three felt people next to each other in one hand. Continue the same process to the fourth, fifth and sixth persons. Hold these three felt people in the other hand.**)*

*(**Lay all six felt people on the rug. Place them next to each other so their hands touch and their love lights show.**) The people all agreed that it was much better to love one another, enjoy their differences and be peaceful people. So they were!*

- Facilitate a discussion with the children about how everyone in the world is different from everyone else. Discuss things like hair color, eye color, skin color and likes and dislikes. Emphasize that one way is not better than another way. All the differences make life more interesting. Point out how boring it would be if all people were the same. Encourage them to appreciate and celebrate the differences in people.

- Bring the Peaceful People follow-up work to the rug. Describe how to make a peaceful person. Select a wall to make a Peaceful People Friendship Chain (people holding hands in a row). Encourage the children to make a Peaceful Person and hang on the wall to be a part of the friendship chain.

- Have the children stand and sing an appropriate song such as *The Colors of Earth.*

- Demonstrate how to pick up the work and take it to the peace shelf. Let them know it will be available for them to do during class time.

- End the lesson by enjoying Silence.

Suggestions for Follow Through:
- Read the book *The Great Peace March* by Holly Near or *All the Colors of the Earth* by Sheila Hamanaka.
- In the classroom add color crayons and/or paints that have a variety of skin tones.
- In ongoing conversations, readings and activities, acknowledge the beauty of diversity.
- Make certain that the work in the classroom reflects diverse genders, races, economics, lifestyles, disabilities, etc.
- Bring in guests that represent diversity.
- Visit places that represent diversity.

Instructions for Making Six Felt Peaceful People:
- Materials needed:
    1) six felt squares in colors that represent shades of skin color (beige, peach, camel, cocoa etc.)
    2) gold glitter glue,
    3) scissors and
    4) marker
- Copy and cut out the pattern on the following page.
- Trace and cut out one felt person from each felt square.
- Place a love light at the heart of each person by making a small circle with the glitter glue.
- Put the six Peaceful People in a basket.

Instructions for Preparing Peaceful People Follow Up Work:
- Place the following materials in a basket.
    1) six colors of paper that represent various shades of skin color
    2) scissors,
    3) either glitter glue or a sticker that can represent the love light,
    4) pencil and
    5) Peaceful Person Tracing Pattern

PEACEFUL PERSON

21

Spirit
The Web of Life

Focus: Self, Community, Cultural and Environmental Awareness

Prerequisites: Activities 1–5

Comments:
This activity provides a visual and concrete way for the children to see and understand the interconnectedness and interdependence of the sun, soil, water, air, plants, animals and humans. The presentation demonstrates that the Earth is not dependent on human beings to exist, but is dependent on human beings to take care of the planet.

Objectives:
• To give children a concrete representation of the interconnection and interdependence of the Earth's elements and life forms
• To increase the children's awareness of the importance of caring for the Earth

MATERIALS

• Two White or Neutral Rugs
• Magic Bag
• Earth Globe
• Web of Life
• Indian Drum (Optional)
• Love Light Pin
• Peace Candle

Preparation:
- Make the Web of Life materials. (See Instructions).
- Place one rug in the center of the circle with the Earth globe in the center.
- Place the basket of the Web of Life in the magic bag. Place the second rug in front of you and lay the drum (optional) and magic bag on top of it.
- Wear your Love Light Pin.

Presentation:
- Greet the children and tell them you have a wonderful activity about Mother Earth that will help them understand how important it is for humans to love and care for the Earth.

- Dramatically reach into the bag and bring out the basket containing the Web of Life. Explain to the children that you have seven felt pieces that represent the seven basic elements and life forms of the Earth. One by one take them out of the basket, name them and lay them on the rug in front of you. (sun, soil, water, air, plants, animals and humans.)

- Invite seven of the older children to participate in the lesson. As you call the children, pin a felt piece on their chests, tell them what part of Earth they are representing and instruct them to hold onto the attached strings. Ask the seven children to sit down in a circle around the Earth globe. Place the person representing the humans to the right of the sun. (You may want to invite the rest of the class to form a larger circle around this small circle so they can see well.)

- Explain to the children that you will go to each of the seven elements to see which ones need each other to exist. Tell the children you will need their help.

- Stand behind the person representing the sun and ask these questions: (It is important to start with the sun, but you do not have to have the circle in this order. Go around the circle left to right from the sun. The human being will be last because he/she is on the right of the sun.)

    1. "Does the soil need the sun?" Answer: Yes
       (Take the end of one of the strings from the person representing the sun and give it to the child representing the soil.)

    2. "Does the water need the sun? Answer: Yes
       (Take the end of one of the strings from the person representing the sun and give it to the child representing the water.)

    3. "Does the air need the sun? Answer: Yes
       (As before, give the end of a sun string to the person representing the air.)

    4. "Do the plants need the sun? Answer: Yes
       (As before, give the end of a sun string to the person representing the plants.)

    5. "Do the animals need the sun? Answer: Yes
       (As before, give the end of a sun string to the person representing the animals.)

    6. "Do humans need the sun? Answer: Yes
       (As before, give the end of a sun string to the person representing the humans.)

- At this point, comment on the fact that all of the elements and life forms need the sun to exist. Reinforce how important the sun is to the Earth.

- Move to the left of the circle and stand behind the next element or life form. Repeat the above questions replacing the word "sun" with the name of the new element or life form.

  1. "Does the water need the soil?" Answer: Yes
     (**As before, give the end of the soil string to the person representing water.**)
     Continue moving clockwise around the circle repeating the questions and connecting the strings.

  2. When you get to the sun and ask the question, "Does the sun need the soil?"
     Answer: "No, the sun stands alone and shares its light and warmth with everything on Earth."

- Continue around the entire circle in this pattern. It is important to emphasize that the sun stands alone and shares its light and warmth with everything on Earth.

- When you get to the human, the pattern changes.

  "Does the water need the humans to exist?"
  Answer: "No, the water could exist without the humans. However, it is important that the humans take care of the water so that it can continue to exist. (**At this point, give the end of one of the strings from the humans to the person representing the water.**)

- Continue around the circle asking the above question and giving the above answer. As you go around the circle, reinforce the idea that humans are guests on the Earth. As you reach each element or life form, briefly comment on some ways that the humans can care for the Earth (recycling, conservation, planting, etc.).

- At this point, the Web of Life is complete. Ask the children to carefully stand up. Reinforce that everything is connected and that the humans must remember to care for and love Mother Earth. Tell the children that you will show them what would happen if humans do not care for the Earth's elements and life forms.

- Move to the person representing water and say, "If humans pollute the water, plants cannot live." (**Pull the water string from the plants.**) Remain behind the person representing water and say, "If humans pollute the water, animals cannot live." (**Pull the water string from the animals.**) Continue pulling the water strings from the elements and life forms in this pattern.

- Move to the person representing air and say, "If humans pollute the air, plants cannot live." (**Pull the air string from the plants.**) Continue pulling the air strings from the elements and life forms in this pattern.

- Continue to move around the circle pulling the strings of each element or life form until the Web of Life collapses. Reinforce how important it is that humans take care of the Earth so that this does not happen.

- Help the children remove the Web of Life felt pieces, wind the yarn strings around their hands and place the felt pieces in the basket. Show them where to place the Web of Life on the peace shelf and invite them to take out the work in the future.

- Have all of the children form a circle around the Earth globe and lead them in an appropriate song about Earth. One suggestion is *The Earth is Our Mother*. A nice addition is to have the children sing the song and move around the Earth globe and the circle to the beat of a drum.

- End the lesson by making Silence and sending love to Mother Earth.

Suggestions for Follow Through:
- During future lessons, go into more detail about how each element affects the other. For example, why does the water need the sun? Why do the plants need the air?
- Draw a seven-sided polygon with a symbolic representation of each of the elements and life forms. Encourage the children to connect the elements and life forms by drawing the connections on paper.
- Continually reinforce the importance of caring for the Earth on a daily basis. Practice this consciously in the classroom by caring for the plants and animals, recycling, conserving paper, etc.
- Encourage children to draw pictures, write stories and do research about the sun, water, soil, air, plants, animals and humans.

Instructions for Making the Web of Life:
- Materials needed:
    1) one felt square of each—gold (sun), brown (earth), light blue (air), dark blue (water), green (plants), rust (animals) and beige (humans),
    2) colored yarn strings to match,
    3) large size jewelry pins,
    4) glue gun,
    5) marker and
    6) scissors
- Cut out each element or life form according to the patterns on the following pages.
- Cut six 4' gold strings for the sun. Cut five 4' strings to match each of the other colors
- Attach the corresponding strings to the back of each felt piece by placing the strings in a row, near the bottom of the felt. Use a glue gun to secure the strings to the felt.
- Glue the jewelry pin to the back of each felt piece.

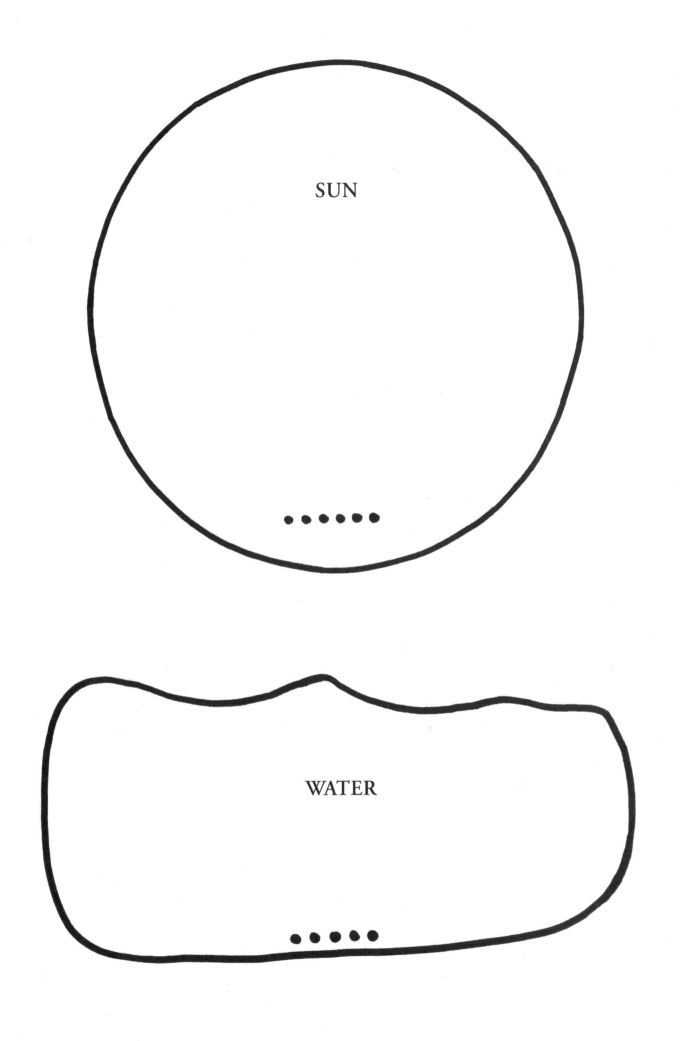

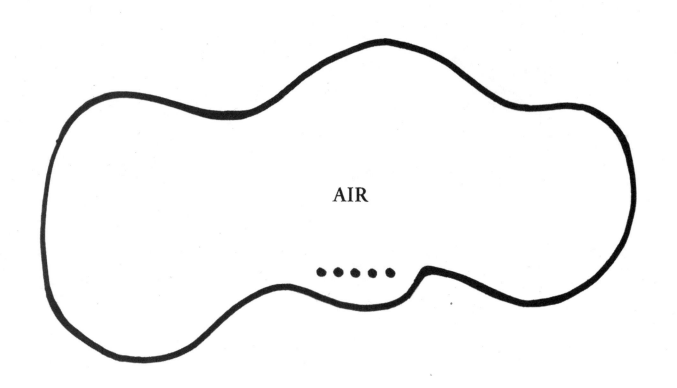

AIR

• • • • •

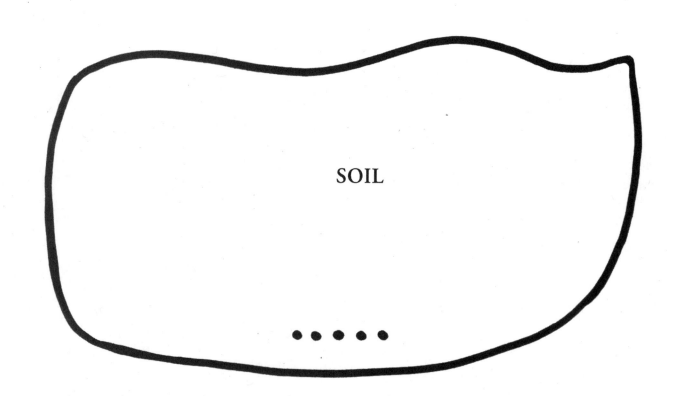

SOIL

• • • • •

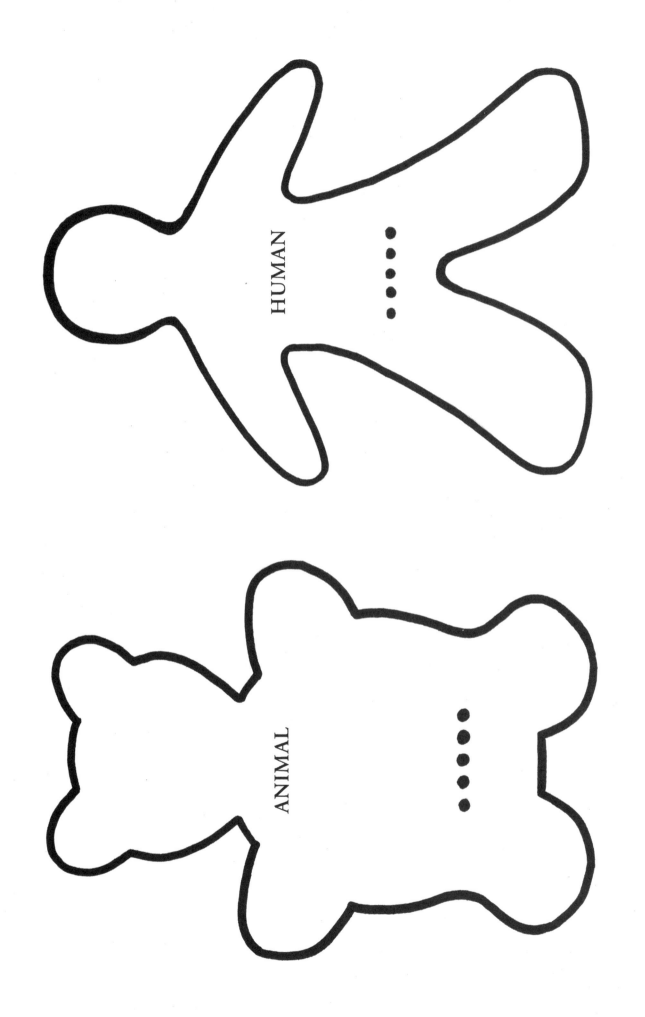

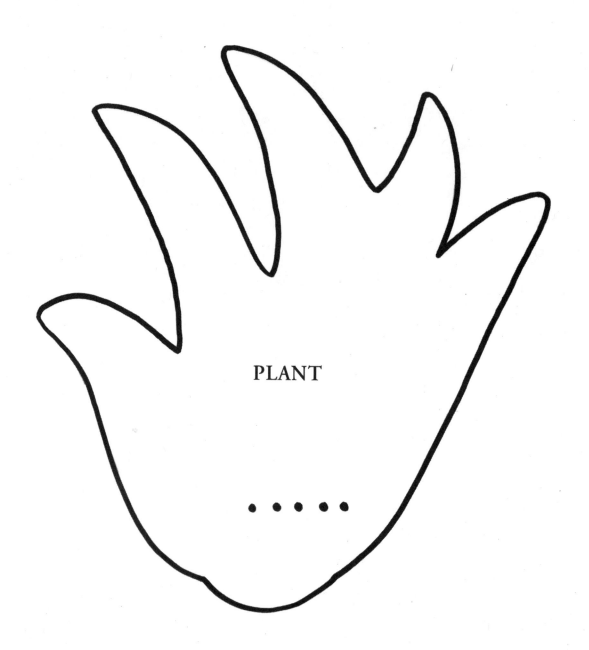

PLANT

. . . . .

22

"I love the confidence these lessons gave my son to be able to face situations that he would face with his friends. He continues to lead and excel in peace."
—PARENT

"The children enjoy using the Web of Love work. They use the small ball for small groups."
—TEACHER

Spirit
The Web of Love

Focus: Self, Community and Cultural Awareness

Prerequisites: Activities 1–3 and 9

Comments:
This activity provides a visual way for the children to share their spirit of love with one another. It works well to repeat this lesson when the class feels like appreciating one another and sharing love. The children enjoy doing it on a spontaneous basis as a part of their ongoing work.

Objectives:
• To provide an opportunity for the children to share their love with one another
• To help the children see how their love is connected

Preparation:
• Make a 4" ball of yellow yarn and a 2" ball of yellow yarn. Place each in a basket.
• Place the Circles of Self Awareness and labels on the rug.
• Place the two baskets of yarn in the magic bag.
• Wear your Love Light Pin.

MATERIALS

• White or Neutral Rug
• Magic Bag
• Circles of Self Awareness & Labels
• One 4" ball of Yellow Yarn
• One 2" ball of Yellow Yarn
• Love Light Pin
• Peace Candle

Presentation:

- Greet the children. Invite them to stand and sing, *This Little Light of Mine.*

- Hold up Circles of Self Awareness and review their names. Hold up the Spirit Circle:

- Tell the children that you will show them a special way to share their love with one another. Dramatically reach into the magic bag and bring out the basket containing the large yellow yarn ball.

- Tell them that the yarn ball will show them how their love is connected like a web.

- Tell the children that you will choose someone in the circle and send him/her love. Explain that you will call out the child's name and say "_____, I am sending you my love." Further, suggest that the person receiving the love say, "Thank you."

- Demonstrate by calling out a child's name, Say "_____, I am sending you my love." Hold onto the end of the yarn and roll the ball of yarn to the person. Encourage the child to say, "Thank you."

- Coach this child to select someone, call out his/her name and say "_____ I am sending you my love." Tell or actually show the child how to put his/her hand on the string to hold it in place and then roll the yarn ball. Encourage the child who received the love, to say "Thank you."

- Repeat this process until every child in the circle has received love. The last child will send it back to you to complete the circle.

- When the Web of Love is complete, ask the children to stand up to see the beautiful Web of Love. Talk about how important it is to share love as it connects us to one another.

- Sing *We Are Flowers in One Garden* or other relevant song.

- Have the children sit down and let go of the yarn. Demonstrate how to roll up the yarn.

- Let the children know that you have one more surprise for them. Reach into the magic bag and bring out the basket with the small yarn ball. Tell them that this yarn ball will be on the peace shelf so groups of children can use it during work time.

- End the lesson by making Silence. Suggest that the children imagine the Web of Love connecting them.

Suggestions for Follow Through:

- Continually refer to the love you feel and see in the children. When you see cooperative activity, comment on the love you can see and feel between them.
- Expand this work to include a compliment each time the yarn ball is rolled.
- Use this activity throughout the year for special occasions and celebrations.

Song Lyrics for *Honoring the Light of the Child* Activities

1. "A Child's Vision"—Sonnie McFarland and Pat Yonka

I am a child with a vision to share, of a world of peace and a world of care.
I so recently came to planet Earth that I remember the peace I had at birth.
Please see my love and nurture me, to make peace on Earth a reality.

2. "This Little Light of Mine"

This little light of mine, I'm going to let it shine. (Repeat three times.)
Let it shine, let it shine, let it shine!

Hide it under a basket—*no!* I'm going to let it shine. (Repeat three times.)
Let it shine, let it shine, let it shine!

Shine it over _____. I'm going to let it shine. (Repeat three times.)
Let it shine, let it shine, let it shine!

3. "Julie's Song"—Julie Fanin

May peace be in you and peace be in me,
The peace that's inside, the peace that's meant to be.
If you shine your light and I'll shine mine too,
Then we'll spread peace the whole world through!

4. "We Are Flowers"—Dave Van Manen

We are flowers in one garden. We are leaves on one tree.
Come and join us. Create peace and harmony! It's a way of life for you and me.

We are pieces of one puzzle. We are people in one group.
Come and join us. Create peace and harmony! It's a way of life for you and me.

We are keys on one keyboard. That's the key to you and me.
Come and join us. Create peace and harmony! It's a way of life for you and me.

5. "Head and Shoulders, Knees and Toes"

Head and shoulders, knees and toes, knees and toes.
Head and shoulders, knees and toes, knees and toes and eyes and ears and mouth and nose.
Head and shoulders, knees and toes, knees and toes.

6. "Dry Bones"

Chorus:
Dem bones, dem bones, dem dry bones; dem bones, dem bones, dem dry bones!
Dem bones, dem bones, dem dry bones—the bones of the skeleton!

The skull is connected to the neck bones; the neck bones are connected to the shoulder bones; the shoulder bone's connected to the arm bones—the bones of the skeleton! Chorus.

The backbone is connected to the hip bones; the hip bone is connected to the leg bones; the leg bones are connected to the foot bones—the bones of the skeleton! Chorus

(For actual scientific names of the skeletal system, go to www.enchantedlearning.com.)

7. "If You're Happy and You Know It"

If you're happy and you know it, clap your hands. (Repeat twice.)
If you're happy and you know it, your body will really show it.
If you're happy and you know it, clap your hands.

The other verses are found on pages 99–102 of this book.

8. "Colors of Earth"—Sarah Pirtle

Chorus:
Who can count all the colors of earth? Each color is different; each color is true.
We are made of the colors of earth, and I love the colors that made you.

Tell me the names of the colors of earth: the purple of eggplant, the purple of peach;
The green and the black of the rocks on the beach and the sun on the mountain in the morning.

When I look in the eyes of my friends, I can see topaz, I can see sky;
The green and the gray of the sea rolling by and the dazzling brown river in the morning.

When I look at the hands of my friends, I can see chestnut, I can see corn;
The color of wheat fields or a dappled brown fawn and the rain-kissed black trees in the morning.

Earth that I love, do you know how I feel? How much I love seashells? How much I love stones?
When I walk barefoot in the fields all alone, I sing out a song to the morning.

9. "Zum Gali"

Chorus:
Zum gali, gali, gali; zum gali, gali! Zum gali, gali, gali; zum gali, gali! Zum gali, gali, gali;
Zum gali, gali! Zum gali, gali, gali, Zum!

Peace is meant for people. People are meant for peace. (English) Chorus

Ha shalom le' man ha amin. Ha amin le' man ha shalom. (Hebrew) Chorus

E' salaamu le e'nasi. E' na suu le' salaam. (Arabic) Chorus

10. "I Walk In Beauty"—Ute—Apache/Navajo

Chorus:
He ne-- ya na------- He ya, he ya na-------- He ne-- ya na----------
He ya, he yo------ He ya, he yo------------------------

I walk in beauty, yes I do, yes I do-------------- I talk in beauty, yes I do, yes I do-------------
I sing of beauty, He-- ne- he-- ne-a-ya, he ya, he yo. Chorus

I weave in beauty, yes I do, yes I do--------------- I sleep in beauty, yes I do, yes I do----------
I dream of beauty, He-- ne- he-- ne-a-ya, he ya, he yo. Chorus

11. "The Earth Is Our Mother"

The Earth is our mother; we must take care of her. (Repeat twice)
Hey Yunga, Ho Yunga, Hey Yun Yun (Repeat twice)
Her sacred ground we walk upon, with every step we take. (Repeat twice)
Hey Yunga, Ho Yunga, Hey Yun Yun (Repeat twice)

12. "What Does Peace Mean?" —Paulette Meier*

(Adaptions: Verse 1, Pat Yonka; Verse 3, Pat Moore's 3–6 class, Giving Tree Montessori School, Detroit, Michigan)

Chorus:

What does peace mean? Peace means taking care of...

What does peace mean? Peace means taking care of ...

What does peace mean? Peace means taking care of ...

Ourselves, each other, and the Earth!

1) When we take care of ourselves, we eat the food we need. We exercise, we play and run. We rest and deeply breathe. We work to grow and learn. We listen with our hearts.

We speak with thoughtful words and know each day's a brand new start.

2) When we take care of each other, we help each other out. We ask each other questions like, "What are you sad about?" We listen to our stories. We take turns in our play.

We cheer each other on as we find our own way.

3) When we take care of the Earth, we listen to her heart. She says, "SAVE THE RAINFORESTS",

'cause that's a very good start. We treasure all Earth's gifts: the air, the sun, and rain.

The worms make soil and help the Earth to breathe and live again.

13. "Come Join the Circle" —Paulette Meier*

Chorus:

Come join the circle. Come join the circle, children.

Come join the circle. Come and join us in the circle. (Repeat.)

In the circle, we're equal. No one is left out. We all can see each other's eyes.

The circle is powerful. It's unbroken. It helps to strengthen all our ties. Chorus

*www.lessonsongs.com

14. "Peace Like a River"

I've got peace like a river, peace like a river. I've got peace like a river in my soul.

I've got peace like a river. I've got peace like a river. Peace like a river in my soul.

(Other verses to be sung as in the first verse)

I've got love like a fire... I've got tears like the raindrops... I've got strength like a mountain....

(Giving Tree Montessori School, Detroit, Michigan, 9–12 verses)

I feel love like the ocean... I feel rough like the ocean... I feel tall as the tree tops ....

(Christian Montessori School, Ann Arbor, Michigan, 12–15 verses)

I've got power like a V-8... I've got hope like a child... I feel bold as the lightning.

References

1. Collopy, Michael. *Architects of Peace—Visions of Hope in Words and Images.* Novato: New World Library, 2000, p.101.

2. *UNESCO and a Culture of Peace-Promoting a Global Movement.* Paris: UNESCO Publishing, 1997, p.255.

3. Ibid. pp. 20–21.

4. *The Hague Appeal for Peace and Justice for the 21ˢᵗ Century.* New York: Hague Appeal for Peace, 1999, p. 13.

5. *UNESCO and a Culture of Peace—Promoting a Global Movement.* Paris: UNESCO Publishing, 1997, pp. 105–109.

6. Montessori, Maria. *Peace and Education.* Adyar: Visanta Press, 1986, pp. 20–21.

7. Ibid. p. 26.

8. Ibid. p. 20.

9. Bradshaw, John. *Healing the Shame. Deerfield Beach*: Health Communications, Inc., 1988, p. ix.

10. McFarland, Sonnie. *Shining Through—A Teacher's Handbook on Transformation.* Denver: Shining Mountains Center, 1993, p. 2.

11. Gibson, Nina. This banner was made by children.

12. Author unknown

13. Montessori, Maria. *The Absorbent Mind.* Oxford: Clio Press, 1988, pp. 57, 60.

14. ———. *The Secret of Childhood.* New York: Ballentine Books, 1966, p. 32.

15. Carey, Ken. *The Third Millenium.* San Francisco: Harper San Francisco, 1991, pp 76–77.

16. Wishon, Phil. "Reflections on Reggio Emillia." *Early Childhood Journal,* Vol 2 Number 1, (Summer 1999), p. 4.

17. Montessori, Maria. *The Secret of Childhood.* New York: Ballentine Books, 1966, pp. 34, 36.

18. Wolf, Aline D. *Nurturing the Spirit in Non-Sectarian Classrooms. Holidaysburg*: Parent- Child Press, 1996, p. 29.

19. Neinhardt, John. B*lack Elk Speaks.* Lincoln: University of Nebraska Press, 1979,

About the Author

SONNIE MCFARLAND began her fascinating journey with children 50 years ago as she became a mother and Montessori teacher within the same year. While wondering what career path would bring her interests and passions together, she found *Montessori's Own Handbook*. Within the first chapter, she knew that she had found her life's work—educating children for peace.

Her career began in Chicago, Illinois where she received the American Montessori Society Primary Credential from the Midwest Montessori Teacher Training Program and taught her first group of children at Northwest Suburban Montessori in Arlington Heights, Illinois.

In 1972, she moved to Pueblo, Colorado and with her husband, Jim, founded the Shining Mountains Center for Education and Consciousness which included a Montessori Children's Center, Adult Education Center and Yoga Center. Sonnie directed and taught at the Shining Mountains Montessori Children Center until she moved to Denver in 1980.

Sonnie joined the faculty at the Montessori School of Denver where she taught children ages 3 to 6 and directed the Montessori School of Denver's Summer Youth Camp for students ages 5–12. During these twelve years, Sonnie created intriguing activities for children that helped them to experience their inner lights of love. As a result children manifested self confidence, joy and peaceful behavior. People visiting Sonnie's classroom often commented on its peaceful feeling and asked her to share her secret.

In 1988 Sonnie began to share this secret when she published an article entitled "Holistic Peace Education" in the *Holistic Education Review*. The article was later included in *New Directions in Education* a collection of the Holistic Education Review's best articles. Following this, she was asked to write the American Montessori Society's Position Paper on *Holistic Peace Education*.

In 1993 Sonnie published *Shining Through—A Teacher's Handbook on Transformation* which outlines activities to help adults center in their love and light so they can see the same in the children. These ideas were reiterated in an article written for the *Montessori Reporter* entitled *The Transformation of the Teacher*. After many years of being asked to describe Peace Education, Sonnie created a holistic model that was described in an article published in *Montessori Life* entitled *Nurturing the Peace Flower—A Model for the Science of Peace*. In 2011 Dr. Jim and Sonnie created a meaningful book for parents entitled *Montessori Parenting: Unveiling the Authentic Self*.

Sonnie's multi-faceted career includes serving as Head of School at the Montessori School of Denver, Board member of the Association of Independent Schools and the American Montessori Society (AMS). She served as the leader of the AMS Peace Committee and was honored as the 2011 Living Legacy Honoree for her work and dedication. Sonnie does teacher education, workshops and consultations across the country on peace education and parenting.

Gift of Books by Sonnie McFarland

For Your Staff, Colleagues, and Friends

ORDER HERE

■ *Montessori Parenting: Unveiling the Authentic Self*
by Dr. Jim & Sonnie McFarland

Qty:_____ $25.00 each $_____

Shipping: $2.00 per book $_____

■ *Honoring the Light of the Child: Activities to Nurture Peaceful Living Skills in Young Children*
by Sonnie McFarland; Peace music by Pat Yonka

Qty:_____ $30.00 each $_____

Shipping: $2.00 per book $_____

■ *Shining Through: A Teacher's Handbook on Transformation*

Qty:_____ $10.00 each $_____

Shipping: $1.00 per book $_____

TOTAL AMOUNT ENCLOSED $_____

Name _____

Organization _____

Please make check payable and return to:

Shining Mountains Press

Address _____

P.O. Box 4155
Buena Vista, CO 81211

City/State/Zip _____

Phone_____ E-Mail _____

For information on workshops, speaking engagements and bulk book orders,
contact Sonnie McFarland at 719-207-2227, email info@ShiningMountainsPress.com,
or visit the website at: **www.ShiningMountainsPress.com**